Diana's Freelance Tips: How to Succeed on Upwork

A Winning 7-Step Formula & Some Hard Truths from a Freelance Pro

By Diana Marinova

Second Edition: November 2016

ISBN-13: 978-1540740717
ISBN-10: 1540740714

CONTENTS

BEFORE WE BEGIN

Working online from home can be a profitable, liberating, and stress-free experience—I know that, and soon you'll know it, too. This book is a step-by-step guide on how to begin and develop a lucrative freelance practice on Upwork. The advice and recommendations I share are practical, actionable, and drawn entirely from my own experience.

What experience, you ask?

At the time of writing this book, I've completed more than forty freelance projects clients have rated with the maximum of five-star reviews for a total of 6,500+ paid hours and even more if counting the hours spent working on fixed-price jobs. My hourly rate was $7 per hour in the beginning, and today it ranges from $40+ per hour for hourly jobs, all the way up to $100+ per hour when working on fixed-price projects.

Most of my work history and client reviews are readily available on my Upwork profile. (A link to my Upwork profile is provided in Appendix 2: URL References. Make sure you are logged in to your Upwork account to see details of both my current and past projects.) You can additionally see my LinkedIn profile (see Appendix 2: URL References) for more feedback from happy clients.

You can also visit my website and freelance marketing blog (see Appendix 2: URL References) to learn more about me and what I do. Browse the 180+ posts filled with freelance and marketing tips, for free. Through my website and blog I have connected with many like-minded people, clients, and fellow freelancers. Readers' questions and pet peeves are honestly what inspired me to write this book in the first place.

Why Upwork, you ask?

At the end of 2013, two of the biggest freelance websites, oDesk and Elance, merged to deliver the most advanced tools for hiring and collaborating online. They invested more in technology and provided more opportunities for businesses and freelancers everywhere. While they kept both websites operational, the newly created company, Elance-oDesk, reported a combined global community of more than eight million freelancers and two million businesses in over 180 countries, with an estimated $750 million in billings in 2013, and growing.

On May 5, 2015 oDesk.com relaunched as Upwork.com and the company management started encouraging Elancers to move their profiles to Upwork in order to take advantage of the platform improvements that were to be implemented in the coming months. In July 2015, the company announced they would be winding down Elance completely. At the end of May 2016, all work on Elance ceased, leaving Upwork as the richest and most advanced marketplace for online work.

According to their <u>about page</u> (see Appendix 2: URL References), Upwork has more than ten million registered freelancers, and more than four million registered clients. This amounts to over a billion dollars' worth of annual work done, and three million jobs posted annually.

This makes it a great place to kick-start your freelance career and my goal is to help you save time and do it right from the first try.

I won't lie to you (ever!) so let me tell you right from the start—this book is not a silver bullet for success. **If you think I'll just serve you freedom and prosperity on a platter, no book can help you.** You will have to *work* to achieve your goals.

Sure, I will give you the steps you need to take to succeed, but don't think for a minute it will be easy. You have to be proactive, especially in the beginning before clients start flocking to you. You have to embrace change as being a freelancer can transform your lifestyle and you might never want to go back to a standard nine-to-five job. You have to commit and work hard—that's the *only* way forward.

Are you ready?

Let's begin.

WHO AM I AND HOW I BECAME A FREELANCER

Hi, I'm Diana and I'm thirty-three years old. I was born in Bulgaria, a beautiful but relatively poor developing country in Eastern Europe.

As a kid, I loved spending time riding my bike, running around the block, and solving mathematical equations. I was really good at playing the violin and won a few regional musical competitions in my country, but after my musical aspirations didn't work out, I discovered my talent for learning new languages, too. I guess that's where my passion for traveling and getting to know new cultures comes from.

Was your childhood anything like mine? Did you find your passion early on in life? Or did you spend years doing things you didn't enjoy only to discover your true calling by accident? Or maybe you are still looking for it? Whatever the case—don't worry. Everyone's different and yet, we all end up wanting the same things or walking the same path.

Whether you are married or not, with or without children, or whether you have a passion for traveling or a preference to stay mostly at home in your comfort zone, I know one thing—if you're reading this book, you want your freedom; you want to regain control of your life; you want to be the master of your time. And you shall be—I know because my story *is* your story; you just don't know it yet.

Now let's fast forward a few years. I had attained a bachelor's degree in public relations and a master's degree in marketing. The academic success led me to the beaten path of the employee: seven years, three countries, and multiple companies later, I was feeling trapped.

Day after day, I had to spend most of my time in the same office, with the same people—Monday through Friday, nine a.m. to six p.m. I had little to no control over the tasks I worked on or the people with whom I communicated and collaborated. I had to put up with unprofessional, and sometimes even insulting, behavior of bosses or clients. I had to pretend it was okay when someone took their bad mood out on me. I didn't have much time for myself, my family, and friends, not to mention the lack of motivation for personal growth.

I wanted so much more from my personal life and career. I wanted time and financial independence to explore the world and pursue my passions.

In late 2009, when the financial crisis hit my home country, I was jobless and almost broke. I had sent hundreds of cover letters for positions I wasn't sure I even wanted. I had gotten a handful of job offers but neither of them met my requirements for work environment, team members, and remuneration package.

For example, I was looking for a marketing management position in an established company, preferably in the travel sector, with a small team who worked well together and treated each other professionally and friendly. I was okay to work full-days provided I had the flexibility to take days off when needed, work from home from time to time, or spend time out of the office on client meetings. I wanted good healthcare, a fair salary, and a remuneration package—e.g. a company car, phone, laptop, and a bonus system for achieving certain goals on a quarterly or yearly basis.

Regretfully, every week I was offered an entry-level job, sometimes in the marketing department, with salary that couldn't pay my rent and bills, no bonus system, or remuneration package of any kind, extra-long working hours with a mandatory presence in the office regardless the amount of work that needed to be done, and a team of people who were more interested in stabbing someone in the back rather than helping them grow in the company or personally.

I was qualified for the positions and companies I wanted, they were simply not hiring because of the financial crisis. Instead, I got job offers from not-so-good employers who were trying to take advantage of the situation.

Right about now, I hear you say—"Wait, what? She got job offers but refused? She wasn't desperate enough … she wasn't hungry enough. No way can I turn my back on paying work."

I hear you, I was thinking the same thing at the time—*do I want too much? Am I asking for the impossible?* I was hungry and desperate. I had some money in the bank to keep me going for a few months, but the money was quickly melting away. To cut costs on food, I ate noodle soup more than once every day for two months.

So yes, I *was* hungry and desperate. But I was proud, too. I had my principles and I wasn't going to compromise on them only because employers wanted to take advantage of me, hiding behind the financial crisis. I was a highly qualified professional, and I wasn't going to work without the pay and work environment I wanted and deserved.

I spent weeks browsing the internet looking for information on alternative employment methods.

One day I stumbled upon a website called oDesk. The feedback from its users was very positive, so I started reading its terms and conditions.

Let me ask you—when you buy a new device or household item, do you study the manual? Most people don't, but unfortunately your freelance career is a little more complicated than a new toaster. It's *not* in your best interest to start applying to projects before getting to know the system and knowing what your rights and duties are as a member of the community. Too many people fail at their attempts to become freelancers simply because they don't read and prepare properly.

Back in the day when I first discovered oDesk, I spent seven days straight reading through the manuals and website rules and procedures. I took my oDesk readiness test, completed my profile, passed some skill tests and started reading through clients' projects.

I was terrified—so many clients, even more freelancers, and every single person fighting for a chance to prove themselves. One job, hundreds of contractors … the competition was killing me. Gladly, I had my marketing background and experience so I approached the whole bidding thing from a different perspective. I didn't bid on as many jobs as I could. Instead, I was trying to position myself as a marketing consultant. I was choosing my prospective clients wisely and offering them proposals they couldn't resist, but I'll detail more on that later in the book.

Still, I spent a week at home, not leaving my desk days and nights, while my friends were out having fun.

I landed my first project only two days after I registered with the website. It was one of the first projects I applied to. Maybe I got lucky, maybe something else, but I am sure this was one of the things that kept me going when I was filled with doubts. It was a miniature English-Bulgarian translation job, but it got me my first $10 and a five-star review on oDesk.

By the way, check the appendix of this book where I detail payment methods suitable for freelancers on Upwork. After all, when you get paid for the first time, you want to be ready to receive your money, right?

Not long after, I got my second project. It wasn't big either, but we all have to start somewhere. It was marketing related and got me eighty more bucks and another five-star review. I was doing it! There was light at the end of the tunnel. I could smell victory. All I had to do is keep at it—and so I did.

It was hard and there were no guarantees. I was reading hundreds of job posts, sending dozens of cover letters and not getting much, if anything in return.

I was picking my clients wisely (discussed in Step 5 of this book) and writing customized cover letters (discussed in Step 6 of this book). So it was taking me a good five hours every day for the first couple of weeks to browse project descriptions, analyze clients, and apply to relevant job posts. With time and practice, I became faster so I was able to complete the same amount of applications in three to four hours a day, which left me time to actually work on the projects I had landed in the meantime.

For the first six months I made half the money I used to make at my last day job. I sent a lot of cover letters, went to many interviews, landed a few projects here and there. I couldn't find employment for forty hours per week, which was the minimum workload at my day job, but freelancing was paying the bills. And I was starting to feel what it meant to have time for myself and to be the master of my own schedule.

Note that at that time I was in Eastern Europe where it's cheaper to live compared to the US, Canada, or developed West European countries. I made about $7,000 the first six months. For the record, I was selling myself short (which I didn't know at the time). If you are good at what you do and you follow the seven steps in this book, you won't have to worry about selling yourself short. You will be able to pay the bills within a few months of your first landed project, no matter where you live.

For the second six months I made twice as much money as in the first six. I was already able to find employment for forty hours per week, but I was quickly realizing I should not be looking for that much work. After all, I had left the nine-to-five job because I wanted to have more time for myself so I could travel and pursue my dreams and interests. If I were to continue working forty hours a week, it would be almost no different than having a day job, and the rat race would consume me again. I had to find a way to work smart, not hard.

So I started raising my prices and cutting the hours I worked for clients. This way, I had enough money to sustain my way of life while freeing up more time to travel and work on my own projects. I didn't call myself a successful freelancer just yet, but I was getting there.

Today, six years later, I can easily fill a forty-hour work week with freelance clients' projects and make over $80,000 per year from Upwork alone—but I choose not to. You know why?

Because I prefer to have more time for myself.

I currently work fifteen to twenty hours per week on clients' projects—one long-term client on Upwork since 2012, the occasional repeat client, and sometimes I take on new short-term clients who find me on Upwork, LinkedIn, or directly through my website.

I spend the rest of my time traveling the world and working on my own projects like blogging, startup ideas, writing books, running coaching programs for freelancers and clients, and developing e-mail training courses.

Actually, at the end of 2013 I achieved a long-held dream of mine by relocating to Spain. I worked from my terrace overlooking the sea in Costa Blanca and became a co-founder of two startups.

I was able to make another long-held dream of mine a reality recently. In early December 2015 my boyfriend and I headed to Southeast Asia, trying to escape the cold winter in Europe. We ended up doing a worldwide trip in six months.

My point being—no matter how little you know about freelance work today, it is possible to use Upwork to achieve financial stability and prosperity in a relatively short period. Sure, success requires you to be good at what you do and to develop certain personal traits and skills (discussed later in the book). But if you do, although a cliché, the sky really *is* the limit when working as a freelancer—you have the freedom to pursue the life *you* desire.

Money is not *that* important. How you live your life *is*.

If you want to earn $100,000 annually as a freelancer—you can. It won't happen overnight and it probably will cost you all the time you have in the day, but you can do it. If having so much money is not important to you, you have other options. You can find a way to ditch the forty-hour work week like I did and be able to enjoy good wine, foreign countries, cultural exchange, long nights out with friends, and living the life your mom and dad never had. **Either way, it starts with the seven steps I'll share with you in this book.**

But be warned—becoming a successful freelancer requires commitment and hard work. I can show you the path but you will be the one to follow it. Don't worry too much though—if you stay positive and persevere, it is only a matter of time before you will get close to your goals and reach them.

Let's take these steps, shall we?

STEP 1: SET YOUR GOALS AND MAKE THEM S.M.A.R.T.

This is the part a majority of freelancers overlook. They never set their goals, let alone make them S.M.A.R.T.

What does this have to do with Upwork?

Bear with me. We'll get there. Before you dive in to the specifics of Upwork, you need to know what you are doing and more importantly, *why* you are doing it. Do you know where you want to be a year from now?

If you don't have goals, chances are you won't achieve what you have in mind. Think about it. If you have no goals, there's no way you can make a good plan simply because you won't quite know the destination you want to reach.

There are some freelancers who do set goals but fail to meet them because the goals were unrealistic, or couldn't be measured, or were way too vague to pursue. So I urge you to set S.M.A.R.T. goals.

S.M.A.R.T. Goals Defined

If you Google the term, you will find many different explanations of the acronym S.M.A.R.T. I will share my favorite one, both for personal and business goals:

- S stands for *specific*

- M stands for *measurable*

- A stands for *achievable*

- R stands for *realistic*

- T stands for *time-based*

Let's see how each of these translates in the context of starting your freelance career.

Specific

Be specific. You may want more clients but don't just set a goal of finding more clients—ask yourself:

- What type of clients—new/repeat, writing/editing, website design/logo design, SMM/e-mail, marketing planning/marketing management, etc.

- How you get those new clients—by bidding on Upwork, by finding them through social media and attracting them to the freelance site, by letting them find you, from referrals, etc.

- How often you evaluate—every month, quarter, or year?

As a general rule of thumb, specific goal setting boils down to answering the Five Ws—who, what, when, where, and why.

Measurable

Make sure you can measure your goals. To continue the example with the new clients, your goal can be ten new clients from Upwork and five of them long-term.

Measurable means you put numbers on it—how many or how much of something you want to achieve.

Achievable

Now that you have made the goals specific and measurable, **it's time to make sure they are achievable, too.** The name speaks for itself—an achievable goal means it is possible for you to accomplish.

If you are just starting as a freelance writer, marketer, designer, etc., you probably won't achieve a $500,000 income during your first year—$10,000 or $25,000 is closer to what you'll be able to do in the first year, depending on how committed you are and how much time you spend on your freelance practice.

When making your goals achievable, answer the simple question of what you are prepared and able to commit to. It is okay for the goals to be challenging and difficult, but make sure they are actually achievable *for you*.

Realistic

The next step is to make your goals realistic. Realistic is pretty similar to achievable. And you can even take an unachievable goal and turn it into a realistic one by stretching its time line.

Let's say you wanted to make an income of $500,000. While you probably won't make it during your first year, you may very well do it in the first five years. So by stretching that goal from one to five years, you make that goal both realistic *and* achievable.

Time-based

Finally, make your goals time-based. If there was a most important ingredient of the S.M.A.R.T. goals, time-based would be it. Put yourself on a schedule. It's okay to change that schedule if your circumstances change but nevertheless, you need to put a deadline for your goals, so that you can start planning how to achieve them.

Examples of S.M.A.R.T. Goals

Find ten new freelance clients on Upwork until the end of December, and at least five of them to hire you on a long-term basis until the end of next June.

Raise your income 20% by the end of Q1 of next year.

Write 50,000 words every month during year X.

Develop your blog and acquire ten clients through it by the end of Q4 of this year

Homework to Set Your S.M.A.R.T. Goals

This homework is simple. Think carefully what you want to achieve in the next twelve months. Take out a blank sheet of paper (or open a new Word document) and do as follows:

- First, write specifics about what is it that you want to achieve—e.g. acquire new clients on Upwork.

- Second, measure your goal—e.g. acquire ten new clients on Upwork by the end of the year.

- Third, make it achievable, realistic, and time-based—e.g. make sure you do have enough time to commit to acquiring those ten new clients on Upwork by the end of the year. If you don't have the time or you think there are not enough good clients in your niche, adjust the details—e.g. five new clients on Upwork by the end of the year, or ten new clients for the next eighteen months on Upwork and LinkedIn.

- Start small with the first requirement and build your way up until you are satisfied with your first S.M.A.R.T. goal.

- Repeat these steps for all the goals you want to set.

- Now write down all your S.M.A.R.T. goals as a list and pin them on your wall or desktop—somewhere handy where you can check them easily if need be.

Revisit these goals monthly or quarterly to check how you're doing. Adjust your plan if circumstances change.

With your goals at hand, it will be so much easier to make all decisions, relating to your success on Upwork. Completing your freelance profile is the next step.

STEP 2: COMPLETE YOUR PROFILE

Your profile on Upwork is what your prospective clients will see when deciding whether to invite you to an interview or move on to the next freelancer. Completing your profile is not a guarantee for success but it's a fundamental—and crucial—part of it. Let's see how to build your profile for success.

Profile Photo

Choose your profile photo wisely. This should be an actual picture of you. Logos, clip art, group pictures, and heavily digitally manipulated images are not allowed on Upwork.

Know that there is no right or wrong choice when deciding about your profile photo—experiment to find what works for *you* to attract *your* target clients.

I would say that a face on your thumbnail helps increase your conversion ratio. Clients like to put a face to the words they read in the proposals they receive. Your niche of expertise should determine the type of photo you use.

For example, if you are a business plan writer, it is somewhat expected of you to be serious and business oriented, right? So a headshot without a smile or just a hint of a smile may be the best choice. Don't be too casual.

If you are a designer for children's books, then a somewhat more artistic photo may be the best option to showcase your personality and creativity.

Feel free to check out <u>Upwork's best practices tips for choosing your profile photo</u> (see Appendix 2: URL References).

By-Line

When I say by-line, I mean that little piece of information that goes with your name on the top of your freelance profile. Upwork currently refers to it as "Job Title".

I have seen many people do different things—some unleash their creativity and put a catchy by-line that hardly ever gives information about what it is that you do—for example: Quality Work Assured.

Others are very brief and to-the-point, giving general information about the niche they work in—for example: Marketing and PR Consultant.

And probably the majority of freelancers choose to share a few of their best-selling services through the by-line: Professional Content Writer| SMO | SEO | Web Development Expert. One of the reasons they do this is to target keywords because website search engines often take into account your by-line.

There isn't any obvious limitation of the number of characters you can put in your by-line, but it is recommended to include a single-sentence description of your professional skills or experience and to keep it to less than ten words.

Like with your profile photo, there is no right or wrong decision when choosing your by-line. Yet there are stronger and weaker ways to construct one.

For example, let's pretend you are a bilingual English and Spanish writer and translator.

If you choose to advertise "Writer and Translator" in your by-line, you will compete with many other writers and translators on the site. But being specific in your by-line by stating "Bilingual English-Spanish Writer and Translator" might help you stand apart from the crowd and appear on top positions when clients perform narrow searches on Upwork.

A by-line can work well for you and not work well for another person with your profession. You should experiment and see what works best for *you* and *your* target clients.

Profile Overview

This is potentially the most important part of your freelance profile because you get to sell yourself in this section. Write it with your desired clients in mind and make sure you describe your goals in detail.

I see mostly two types of Upwork profile overviews— one is focused entirely on the freelancer, and the other one is focused entirely on the client's needs, following all marketing copywriting rules. Neither will work as well on Upwork as would a combination of the two approaches.

Don't tell the story of your life in your profile overview. Furthermore, don't repeat your employment or education details—there are separate sections for those on your profile. Instead, focus on what you are good at, what you want to do, and why they should hire *you*.

If you've ever taken any marketing or copywriting course, you know how important it is to focus on benefits over features. It's true clients will hire you not because you are great at your job, but because your greatness at your job will solve their problem.

However, after many experiments with my Upwork profile and after working with different freelancers from various professions, I recommend combining the two approaches for the profile overview—lead with some information about yourself and close with the client-focused information of why they need to hire *you*.

Why should your Upwork profile overview be self-focused while at the same time also speaking to the client's needs?

This matters because of the stage of the decision-making process your prospects are at when searching for freelancers on Upwork.

A profile overview that focuses the client on the benefits you can provide to their business would be suitable for people who know they need help but are not quite sure what they need. A value-focused copy will help them realize their problem and find out what solution they need.

However, people who search freelancers on Upwork often have a very clear idea of not only their problem, but also of the solution they are seeking. Therefore, they are looking for a very specific set of skills or services. In this case, an entirely value-focused profile overview is more likely to come across as marketing fluff text rather than useful information.

Clients on Upwork most often don't need information about their problems or convincing what solution they need. They already know that.

They need convincing why it is *you* they need to hire. That's why leading with a bit of information about yourself will go a long way to grabbing their attention when communicating what type of person you are and if you are the right fit for their team.

Figure out your unique selling proposition *and* your value proposition.

If you don't know what these marketing terms are:

Your unique selling proposition (USP) is what differentiates you from your competition—that single thing that nobody else offers or does as well as you do.

And your value proposition is what's in it for your client; what your client gets out of hiring you (and from your unique selling proposition in particular).

Let me give you an example.

Let's say you write great blog posts with high quality, deliver them on time, work openly with editors, and gladly do edits when requested. Unfortunately, so do hundreds maybe even thousands of other freelance bloggers. Why hire *you*?

Because of your USP and more importantly, because of your value proposition.

In the above example, your USP can be your incomparable expertise writing search-engine optimized blog posts on print advertising topics.

Your value proposition on the other hand could be 500 targeted visitors within the first three days of publishing your post for a highly competitive keyword because of your search engine optimization (SEO) expertise and established authority as an author in the print advertising niche.

Here are a few other examples of possible USPs and value propositions, regardless of your profession:

USP 1: Preliminary thirty-minute *free* call to discuss with your prospect their target audience profile and *their* value proposition.

Value Proposition 1: Your client doesn't start paying until you have the big picture and confirm you can do the job with the required quality, within the said time frame and budget.

USP 2: Asking the right questions at the right time.

Value Proposition 2: Your client is sure that you will always work in the right direction because you never assume anything—you work only when knowing what is required of you and why, which saves them time and money in the long-run (no re-work is ever needed).

USP 3: You do free preliminary research and get acquainted with all existing marketing materials to make sure your materials (content, design, etc.) deliver the same message everything else does.

Value Proposition 3: Your client has the confidence that you will keep their brand integrity and clients' loyalty through consistency in broadcasted messages and company values.

Add your profession and skills to provide some context and you will narrow down these USP and Value Proposition examples and make them specific. *The bottom line: every USP can and should be translated into a value proposition.* If you have an excellent USP but the client doesn't care for it, your value proposition will be weak and they will still not hire you.

Make your profile overview personal—clients hire people, not robots. Don't use too many words but make it detailed enough. Two or three paragraphs usually work fine. If needed and appropriate, use bullet points to make it easy to read through your skills or expertise.

And remember—the client who reads your Upwork profile overview wants to know what's in it for them, but he or she also wants to know who you are even more.

There are many people who can do the job you do. But there is only one you—your profile overview is where you communicate who you are and what you bring to the table, should you be hired—in terms of both professional and personal skills. Let your personality shine.

Let me show you how I write profile overviews by following the tips I just shared.

Disclaimer: these are not real people and the provided profile overviews are just for illustration purposes. The information in them may or may not be accurate in terms of needed qualifications to perform a certain task or job. These profile overviews are in no way to be copied or reprinted without prior confirmation from me.

Mark is a thirty-year-old nutritionist and fitness buff. He likes reading and writing, too. He has a lot of spare time and wants to make a living as a freelance writer online.

I'm a good nutritionist and I have a deep passion for writing. I love to share my expertise and motivate people to improve their lives by getting in shape and changing their eating habits. You should definitely get in touch with me if you need:

- Healthy eating recipes for your blog or nutrition website

- Ghostwriter for your next e-book on healthy eating or getting in shape

- A review of your healthy product (food or fitness related)

- Content for your nutrition or fitness website, converting readers into paying customers

- A series of e-mails to grow your e-mail list and build a community of loyal subscribers

- Articles, blog posts, white papers and anything about healthy eating or fitness!

I have never missed a deadline in my life. I reply to e-mails within one business day. I eat healthy and go to the gym three times per week. I am an old-time subscriber of many nutrition magazines and websites, including *Today's Dietitian*, *Food & Nutrition* magazine, and *Men's Health* magazine. My wife swears I would have made an excellent chef, too!

My passion for healthy eating and having a healthy body, combined with my writing talent, makes me a perfect fit for most writing gigs in the nutrition and fitness niches. So why look elsewhere? Contact me now so we can further discuss your project needs and how I can help you.

Jane is a twenty-year-old college student with great artist skills. Ever since she was a little girl, she wanted to be a graphic designer. She has helped many of her friends' parents create logos for their startups, brochures for their family businesses, newsletters, and more. Finally, she decided to start making money off her designer's talent, even though she was still in college.

When I was five, I asked Santa Claus for a special painting set that could create all the colors in the world. As I grew, so did my skills and passion for drawing. Today, I am a college student majoring in graphic design at University X. What most people find hard, including design students and accomplished designers, comes naturally to me—visual thinking. It's easy for me to find the perfect combination of colors, simplicity, and shapes to bring your thoughts to life in a visual way.

There is still a long way to go before I can say I am an accomplished artist and qualified graphic designer. But with over a hundred complete fun projects, helping family and friends, I invite you to browse my portfolio. You can find my designs for print as well as online mediums (business websites, personal blogs, magazines, and more).

I will be a great fit if you need:

- Children's book illustrations

- Website and blog design

- Illustrations for your company marketing collateral materials—be it a website, blog, print brochure, media kit, newsletters or just some original

Thanksgiving cards to send to your clients

I am in the process of learning the ropes of logo design, mobile app design, and motion graphics design. Aside from my classes in college, I am available to work on clients' projects. I am sensitive to deadlines (which cannot be said for too many designers out there).

I have been told repeatedly I am a fresh breeze for every creative department. So should you contact me to discuss a project, I can promise you original ideas and designs which not only your target audience would love, but designs which achieve exactly the goal you asked me to achieve.

Pamela is fifty-five years old. She used to be the VP of Marketing in a big company but after many years of managing large teams, she decided it was time to leave behind the responsibilities of a VP and start something of her own; something equally rewarding but without as many responsibilities and stress.

Pamela has always loved the ever-changing world of marketing and technology. Naturally, social media seemed like a nice change of pace. So she became a social media marketer for hire.

After thirty years in the corporate world, today I enjoy the peaceful and fulfilling life of a freelance social media marketer. With my knowledge and expertise, I can help you connect with your target audience through various social media channels. I can show you and teach you how to build a healthy relationship with your communities for better ROI of your business.

I bring to you many years of experience both in corporate marketing and management. But also, I can offer you advice and much needed guidance in growing your business in today's uncertain and ever-changing digital landscape. It has never been more important to be curious and flexible than in today's world when everyone has access to everything at their fingertips through computers and mobile devices.

Maybe you've heard people don't buy on social media. Be that as it may, I will help you build such a healthy relationship with your target audiences that you'd never have to sell anything to anyone. They would love spending time with you online and will come running to you every time you release a new product or service.

I like crunching numbers so rest assured that no report would be left unanalyzed. Your goal is my goal. I have the hands-on experience to set goals and draw you a roadmap for success on networks like Facebook, Twitter, LinkedIn, YouTube, Pinterest, Google+, and more. Also, I have the analytical thinking to tweak the strategy and tactical plan as needed to achieve long-term ROI from social media activities.

I can create a strategy that fits your business needs; I can manage your social media accounts; or I can train you to do it yourself. I don't offer a one-size-fits-all type of social media marketing. Everything I do is tailored to you and your specific business needs and goals.

If you want to bring your business into the twenty-first century and start connecting with your target audience in a meaningful way to improve your KPIs, contact me today!

And finally, make sure your profile overview starts strong. You have ten seconds to capture your prospect's attention, so make your first sentences count.

Video

Upwork offers the opportunity to add a video to your profile. Upload your video to YouTube, paste its URL in the designated field, and you're done. Please see the site's requirements for the videos (see Appendix 2: URL References).

Note that adding a video is not always recommended. Add a video only if you feel comfortable doing it or when it will add value to your profile.

For example, if you are trying to land sound recording, customer service, or other types of projects which would require excellent diction in English, you can use your video to show that to your prospective clients before they even decide to contact you.

If you are after projects which would require you to make cold calls or talk to people and convince them of something, you can show your personality and style in your video to attract more clients, too.

If you are a motion graphic designer, you can use this section to add video samples of your work (it's not necessary for you to be in the video you add).

For other freelancers though, adding a video to their profile may work against them.

For example, if you are not fluent in English or you have a heavy accent, making it difficult for prospects to understand what you say, you are better off not uploading a video. You may be brilliant at what you do but if you speak to them in broken English, they won't give you a chance.

Another example I'd like to give is related to the way you like working. If the work you are interested in doesn't have to do much with live communication and you certainly don't like showing your face or participating in live video conference calls—then don't upload a video. If you intend to never have a video call with a client, be consistent and don't give them a video preview of yourself on your profile.

By the way, I am one of those people—I have never uploaded a video of myself on Upwork, and it never stopped me from getting clients. I have excellent reviews on the site, over 6,500 work hours and more than forty projects—all without a video on my profile.

Adding a video to your Upwork profile is optional. Due to the proprietary information of their algorithms, Upwork doesn't reveal statistics about the exact percentage of freelancers who add videos to their profiles. The site support team was kind enough though to share some info on the topic.

According to Upwork, not many freelancers add a video on their profiles. Video is mostly added by high performing freelancers, mainly among freelancers who work in the Design & Multimedia and IT & Programming categories.

So adding a video to your profile may help you stand apart from the crowd, but not adding one certainly doesn't mean you don't stand a chance. You can stand out in other ways, too. Make sure you add a video *only* because you want to and because it could aid your success. Not because someone else told you so.

Specialties

Remember how you focused your profile overview toward the clients you *want* to attract? Build on that and list relevant specialties.

For example, if you want to land search engine optimization (SEO) projects, list skills like keywords research, onsite SEO, content marketing, blog management, and so on.

If you want to be hired as a marketing consultant, list your skills about marketing planning, business planning, strategy consulting, content strategy and management, and so on.

If you want to land designing projects, list the type of design you specialize in—web design, logo design, branding materials, etc.

If you want to grow as a WordPress developer, don't tell your prospective clients how good you are with Drupal. Focus on the WordPress development skills you possess—e.g. plugin creation, WordPress theme creation, popular theme customization like Genesis, Thesis, Woo themes, or other themes you are familiar and experienced with, and so on.

If you are after editing gigs, don't tell them how good of a writer you are. Focus on your editing skills—e.g. are you well versed with American or British English, or both; what editing style you follow; whether you offer copyedit only or also critique of manuscripts; what responding styles do you offer to your clients, and so on.

Use the specialties section to focus your clients on the skills you want to be hired for.

Professional Experience and Education

This may be trivial, but these sections are important. There are still people who prefer working with freelancers with more experience or higher education, so be sure to mention everything you've worked and studied. You never know who might be reading and hiring.

But again—don't tell the story of your life. List the experience and education that relate to what you actually want to be hired for. If you want to land editing gigs, your past experience as a waiter or a waitress won't do you any favors. Don't include it.

If you want to be hired as a project manager, including your past experience as a tour leader or a travel guide can actually prove helpful—organizing a day for a group of forty or more people will testify to your superb time management and organizational skills, all too needed in the daily work of a project manager.

When you list your experience, make sure you focus it not so much on what you have done but how that would help your potential client.

Nobody would care that you have been on ten trips to the Grand Canyon during the past five years. But prospects will be impressed when you tell them that during your ten trips to the Grand Canyon, all 1,500 tourists left five-star reviews about you and your travel agency because your program was well organized, everything was running smoothly on time, and nobody fell off the cliff under your management.

Remember—clients hire you for the benefits they'll get, not because you are super good at what you do.

Portfolio

I am not talking about your freelance portfolio in general. There's a profile section on Upwork called

"Portfolio." That is what I refer to when I mention your portfolio in this book.

Similarly to the skills and previous experience sections, **use your portfolio to showcase the skills you want to be hired for**. Focus on the areas where you want to grow.

If you want to be hired as a blogger on marketing topics, don't include your culinary blog posts and recipes. If you want to do logo design, probably that awesome billboard design you did that one time won't do you much good.

Organize your portfolio properly. Sure, you do marketing and it includes a lot of tasks like social media marketing (SMM), e-mail marketing, press release writing, strategy writing or daily management. Separate those in different folders and make sure every prospective client can easily and quickly find exactly what they want—be it social media, e-mail, press release, or other marketing material you have chosen to showcase.

Your Profile in the Long Term

In the beginning, you won't have any prior reviews from satisfied clients, so you will have to actively look for projects to work on. But after the first few successfully completed projects, clients will start finding you when doing their search on Upwork. They will be the active party. They will be approaching to ask if you can have a look at their project and if you can make some time to help them.

Design your profile the way I suggest in this section of the book and you may never *have to* look for a client again. You will be declining most of the invites you get and accepting only those which are really interesting to you and pay well. Feel free to tweak the details in certain parts of your profile (e.g. specialties, strengths, etc.) as time passes and your experience grows or preferences change.

Homework to Build Your Profile for Success

- Write down what you want to do as a freelancer—be detailed and specific.

- Picture your perfect clients—who they are and what they want.

- Write down what you have to give them and why they should hire you to give it to them.

- Decide what your profile picture should tell your prospects about yourself.

- Choose your best work to include in your portfolio on your profile.

- **Now go build your perfect profile on Upwork.com—remember it is all about what you want to do and whom you want to work with.**

STEP 3: TAKE RELEVANT SKILL TESTS

In the early stages when you don't yet have any projects or positive feedback from clients on Upwork, you can take skill tests to showcase your skills. Skill tests results are one of the factors potential clients weigh when deciding on interviewing a starting freelancer without proven track record (or not).

How to Take Skill Tests

Skill tests on Upwork are free and available to all.

Before you get started with each test, you can view its syllabus. Once you click the start button, the system generates your test and allows a certain time for completion. Usually, the overall time for each test is forty minutes. Once started, you need to finish in one session—saving and returning to a certain question is not possible.

You have between thirty seconds and one and a half minutes to answer each question. The time for each question is different, depending on its complexity. There is a timer at the top of the test window, showing how much time you have left to answer the specific question.

There is a minimum score you need to achieve to pass each test. If you fail a test or don't like your score, you can make the test result private—so don't worry about embarrassing yourself. You can also retake the same test after one month.

The higher your score, the better the impression you will make. Upwork has a system in place to reward freelancers who pass skill tests with flying colors. If you take a test with better results than 90, 80 or 70% of the people who have ever taken the test, you will earn a badge for being in the top 10, 20, or 30 percentile. It will visually differentiate you from the rest of the freelancers who apply for the same job.

What Skill Tests to Take

A common pet peeve for starting freelancers on Upwork is figuring out what tests to take and how many of them. Provided you will be working online and the communication will happen most likely in English, I'd say the skill tests can be divided in two groups—English skills tests and professional skill tests.

English Skill Tests

Should you or should you not take English skill tests? The answer is it depends.

There are many and different English skill tests such as basic English, vocabulary, UK vs US spelling, English sentence structure, proofreading and editing (Chicago, AP, Oxford style), creative writing, technical writing, blogging, etc.

If you make your living writing content—then yes, obviously English skill tests are kind of mandatory.

Clients on Upwork more often (if not always) prefer writers who have passed the required tests with a good score instead of freelancers who have barely passed or did not take the skill tests at all.

For every other non-content-writing profession, English skill tests are a bit redundant. A single test demonstrating your basic English skills would be enough to convince the client there's no language barrier.

Professional Skill Tests

My experience lies with content writing, marketing, and management skill tests on Upwork. They were all of high quality and show somewhat realistically the freelancer's knowledge of the subject matter. I found some of the tests to be focused too much on the theoretical knowledge and not on real life examples or problem solving by putting that knowledge into practice.

Let's say you have aced your class for market research. As a result you know marketing terms and the methodology to do a market research. In theory you know how to approach the problem, how to build your research, what metrics to take into account and why, and so on. But you have never conducted market research in your life.

You have your knowledge from your classes and the skill tests will assess that knowledge. You will pass the test, although you have never practically done any market research.

Nevertheless, the available skill tests are a good way for potential clients to decide how knowledgeable an applicant is so take your time and take the tests you think will highlight your strengths as a freelance professional.

I would recommend taking as many professional skill tests as possible, especially if you are just starting.

Having said this—no skill test is mandatory, but let's put it like this:

If you have taken some skill tests with a good score, it could drastically increase your chances of landing your first freelance gig on Upwork. Remember—take professional skill tests which relate to the area of expertise you want to be hired in. No need to take a Photoshop skill test if you are writing press releases.

When to Take Skill Tests

I'd recommend taking a few skill tests in your niche of expertise before you even start applying to projects. After that you can take as many tests as you want, whenever you want. I myself take additional tests from time to time, when a new test is released, or if a prospective client requires all candidates to take a certain test, which I have not yet taken.

If you apply to a project and the client requires a specific test don't ignore the requirement. Don't say you'll take the test later. Don't think of different scenarios when you would need or won't need to take the test. Just take it. If you don't, chances are the client will dismiss you as a candidate who can't follow instructions and is not willing to make an extra step to land the job.

If the client has put a test as a requirement, probably that was one of his or her filters to short-list candidates out of tens or even hundreds of job applicants. If you have not taken that test, the client would more likely ignore your application and not read your proposal than giving you a chance to take the test later.

Don't Try to Game the System

There are plenty of websites online, offering Upwork test answers for free. Don't use them. Take your skill tests honestly.

Sure, you can easily find the correct answers online and take the test to score the highest results possible. But if you cheated on the test, what good is that for you? **Passed skill tests are of no use to you if you don't actually possess the skills.**

If a client hires you based on your skill test results and you fail to deliver because you lack the skills that will only result in poor feedback and wasted time. Your reputation is the only thing that matters—don't put it on the line by cheating on the test. Instead, spend some time to master a skill and take the test honestly. If you fail, study some more and try again until you pass the test with flying colors for real.

Five Points to Remember about Skill Tests

- **Taking the basic English skills test is recommended but not mandatory.** Even if you are a native speaker, take this test—too many contractors out there pretend to be native English speakers so you want to make sure in advance your prospective clients know you know English.

- **If you are a freelance content writer, you should definitely take as many relevant English and writing skill tests as possible.** There are no tests to assess your expertise in a certain niche, rather tests to assess your knowledge of the English language in terms of spelling, grammar, sentence structure, and types of writing (e.g. creative, fictional, blogging, technical, etc.)

- **If you are another type of freelancer (not a content writer), it is recommended you take the skill tests which are relevant to your profession.** For example, if you are a graphic designer, take Photoshop, Illustrator, CorelDraw, AutoCAD, or any other available specialized test to showcase the graphic design skills and knowledge you possess. If you are a financial consultant, go to the financial and accounting category of skill tests and see which skill tests apply to your niche of expertise. Take those.

- **Skill tests are of crucial importance when building your freelance profile** and applying to job posts, especially if you don't have any completed projects and feedback on Upwork. The more and relevant tests you take, the better.

- **The score you pass the test with is also very important.** Passing a test with flying colors in the top percentile visually differentiates you from competing freelancers.

Homework to Get Started with Skill Tests

Now that you know what clients you want to work with and what projects you want to land, browse the available skill tests in your niche and note down five you should take first. Then start taking one test a day.

Technically, you can take them all the same day, but as I mentioned earlier, the skill tests truly reflect the level of knowledge and skills you possess. So beware—probably you will get tired after a test or two and when you are tired, you can score poorly because you were tired, not because you didn't possess the skill.

Remember that each test takes about forty minutes to complete. Pace your efforts and take one skill test per day. In five days, you will have taken all five you deemed necessary to be taken before you start applying to projects.

STEP 4: POSITION YOURSELF AND CALCULATE YOUR PRICES

Setting your freelance prices the right way will help you position yourself on the market. With your unique selling proposition and value proposition at hand, you are already one step ahead of the competition. You are ready to get hired by the *right* clients. But how do you make them trust you and award their project to *you*?

Competition Research

Research your competition to find your place on the market—what skills are in demand? Which of your skills are in high demand or with scarce supply? What are the average prices of freelancers with similar background and experience to yours? And so on.

On Upwork, this research should be fairly quick and easy to do. Look for the following:

- What are the average, and more importantly, the most common rates on the profiles of freelancers who offer similar services?

- Is there an obvious correlation between freelance profile rate and freelancer's location?

- What part of the freelancers in your niche of expertise are from India, the Philippines, Pakistan, and other geographical places with a relatively low standard of living where the majority of freelancers price themselves on the low end?

- What's the significance of the proven track record (reviews or lack of such) on Upwork when it comes to profile hourly rate?

- What is the correlation (if any) between the freelancer's profile rate and their niche of expertise—broad area of services or strictly specializing in something; independent contractor or part of an agency team; operative or management skills; what else?

A very important note I'd like to make to readers who are located in any of the above mentioned countries— these questions do *not* suggest you should price your services at the low end only because you are located in a low socioeconomic country. The purpose of the above questions is only to gather information about your competition; to see patterns which are evident on the market, if any, and use them to your advantage. Let's see how to do that.

To show how answering these questions will help you get to know your competition, I conducted research in the <u>Sales & Marketing category of Upwork</u> (see Appendix 2: URL References).

My first step was to find the top marketing skills in demand. I opened the <u>Sales & Marketing category</u> to see what jobs were available (see Appendix 2: URL References).

Note that by the time you read this book, the top marketing skills in demand on Upwork may or may not be the same as outlined here. However, whatever the skills in demand are at any given moment, this sample research will give you the principles and will help you find *your* skills in demand so you can break through and make a name for yourself.

During my research, I saw two of the subcategories had a significantly larger amount of job posts than the rest. Those were SMM (Social Media Marketing) and SEO (Search Engine Optimization).

So, if I were an expert in any of these fields with a proven track record, it would enable me to price myself higher than the average rate because those skills were already in demand.

Let's look deeper in each of these categories.

Thanks to the <u>search engine on Upwork</u> (see Appendix 2: URL References), I managed to see quickly that the profile rates of freelancers offering social media marketing services were two, even three times lower, than the business consultancy and marketing planning rates.

This was partly because a lot of social media marketers were from countries with a low socioeconomic status. The other (and I think more important) factor was that there were not so many people on Upwork who could offer strategy planning and high-level business consultancy.

To put it in other words, many contractors for hire could do low-level social media activities or manage small business day-to-day SMM activities. But very few people could make a social media strategy plan for a business and then monitor and analyze the results, tweak the strategy as they went, train a marketer to do the daily work, and so on. Even fewer were those who could integrate social media with other communication channels as part of the overall business strategy. For that reason, such consultants could sell their services and skills at much higher rates than the average freelancer.

To add some numbers in the mix, I observed the first group of operative social media marketers charged from $3 to $10 per hour for low-level SMM. They were mostly from low socioeconomic countries and could do very simple tasks under strict supervision. Social media marketers who could manage clients' SMM accounts independently charged $10 to $20 per hour. The price was the same for virtual assistants who offered SMM services as part of their overall assisting packages. Then there were the SMM strategy planners who charged $20 to $50 per hour, depending on their experience and expertise. And finally, the integrated marketing strategists who offered SMM strategy planning as part of larger business consultancy packages—they charged $50 to $150 per hour.

The picture in the SEO category is quite similar. Back in the day, link building used to be a big hit on oDesk (now Upwork). Search engines have gotten smarter today though, and backlinking is not quite a viable option for businesses. Nevertheless, there are still plenty of freelancers on Upwork offering such a service.

During my competition research in the SEO category, I noticed the most common price for link building started at $5 per hour and went up to $7 or $8 per hour. Freelancers who offered link building services most often were located in India, Pakistan, and Bangladesh, which additionally kept the prices low.

Prices for SEO went as high as $15-35 per hour if the freelancer provided more complex and actual search engine optimization work like quality keywords research, competitors' links profile analysis, and SEO audit and implementation. Like in the SMM category, at the highest end of the spectrum, I found the marketers, who offered SEO as part of larger business consultancy packages.

Also, I noticed prices are influenced by the freelancer's location—the more developed the country where the freelancer lives, the higher his or her profile rate. And finally, on which end of the price range you put yourself depends on factors like native language, English fluency, experience, specific skills, availability, proven track record, and more.

In addition, my research revealed clearly four types of correlation that can be used when forming your pricing strategy:

1. **Between reviews and profile rate:** The more reviews and positive feedback you have, the higher price you can sell your services at.

2. **Between completed jobs and profile rate:** The more work you have done on Upwork, the more new clients are inclined to trust you and hire you for their project at a higher rate.

3. **Between location, specialization and profile rate:** People in India, Pakistan, the Philippines, and Egypt, among others, have the lowest hourly rates while people in the US, Canada, and UK have the highest profile rates. The profile rates of European freelancers are somewhat balanced, depending on their niche. The level of their specialization appears to be more important than their location when forming their prices. The same is valid for Russia and former Soviet Republics. *Remember this is just an observation of a pattern on the market; it is **not** advice to charge low rates if you are located in a low socioeconomic country.*

4. **Between profile rate and amount of fixed-price jobs:** Freelancers with higher hourly rates on their profiles do more fixed-price projects, which is understandable. Their higher hourly rate implies they have extensive experience and their skills are in high demand. So they prefer to get paid for their work, not for their time; for the value they bring, not for the time they spend working.

Which leads me to my next point when looking for your place on the market—how you get the client to hire you.

Benefits for Your Clients

In order to get hired, focus on the benefits you bring to your clients, not on your strengths as a freelancer, and definitely not on your hourly rate. **Value beats price every time.** It's true for every single client who will hire you for your skills. And only those clients who hire you for your skills are the *right* clients for you.

So don't pitch your clients with your price in mind, approach them with what's in it for them. Remember the example I gave you earlier when you were writing your profile objective and figuring out your USP and value proposition?

Your clients are not hiring you because you write great blog posts with high quality, deliver them on time, work openly with editors, and gladly do edits when requested.

They are hiring you because you can deliver 500 targeted visitors within the first three days of publishing your post for a highly competitive keyword because of your SEO expertise and established authority as an author in the print advertising niche.

And they are definitely not hiring you because you charge $100 per hour (or whatever hourly rate you decide to price your services at). This doesn't mean you can't get them to hire you at that price though.

Successful business owners will always look for ways to cut their costs, but they will never compromise with quality over a price dispute. They respect their freelancers. They know they get what they pay for. If they don't, they will learn it soon enough the hard way and will come running back to you when they know it. In the meantime, stand your ground during price negotiations and don't succumb to the requirements of lesser clients to lower your prices.

Don't sell yourself short—know what you're worth and stand by it.

Successful business owners (a.k.a. good clients) don't pay you for the hour you spend working. They pay you for the years of education and experience you have under your belt that enables you to do your job so well in an hour. So believe in yourself, stand straight, and ask for what you deserve. Where you live has nothing to do with any of it!

Minimum Hourly Rate/Profile Rate

Many clients on Upwork don't publish their projects publicly but look through available freelancers on the platform and invite them to an interview. One of the factors they take into account when doing that is your profile rate. They would expect your service to be in the price range of your profile rate, should you accept the interview.

For that reason, you should put your minimum hourly rate as your profile rate—the rate under which you will never ever accept a job offer. Depending on the project specifics, you can always change the rate during the negotiations to reflect the specific project scale or complexity of the tasks involved. But it's important you set the bar correctly.

Here's a quick formula you can use to calculate your minimum hourly rate:

((personal expenses + business expenses + other expenses) / hours worked) + tax %

This formula will give a different result to everyone because we all live differently. Also, location heavily impacts our living costs as well as due taxes. And let's not forget that the minimum hourly rate for a starting freelancer naturally is lower than for an experienced freelancer with a proven track record whose skills are in high demand.

To show you how to use this formula, let's see how it applies for me at the moment.

Personal expenses—this is the money I need to pay my rent and bills, buy food, clothing, and alike. For me it's roughly $10,000 per year.

Business expenses—these would include software licenses and recurring payments, internet bill, office space (if you don't work from a home office), accountant services, and alike. For me it's roughly $3,000 per year.

Other expenses—put here anything that is not of necessity for your well-being right now but you either want to have it, or will need it later in your life. For example, massage or a beauty procedure on a regular basis, maintaining a car, skiing as a hobby during winter months, a travel fund to cover expenses for a monthly trip, retirement fund or other savings, etc. I put in this section also the fees I need to pay for getting paid—e.g.

Upwork, PayPal and bank fees. For me these other expenses amount to roughly $30,000 per year.

Hours worked—if you intend freelancing to be your single source of income, you can decide how many hours a week you want to put in to work on clients' projects. There are plenty of successful freelancers who work forty or more hours a week. There are many who choose to work only a few hours every week. I am at the stage when I work about fifteen hours on clients' projects, and I usually do so for fifty weeks per year. (I travel so much that I rarely go on a vacation without my laptop and without doing anything for clients; I simply can't make myself stay away.) This amounts to 750 hours per year.

Tax—as I said, this is something which relates to your location as laws and regulations differ from country to country and from one type of entity you operate under to another. Let's say taxes are roughly 20%.

So now we have the following formula:

((personal expenses of $10,000 per year + business expenses of $3,000 per year + other expenses of $30,000 per year) / 750 hours worked) + 20% tax

This makes my minimum hourly rate $68.80/hour. This is the minimum hourly rate I have for new clients right now. Should my living situation change in some way, e.g. higher rent, more business expenses, desire to work less hours on clients' projects, etc., my minimum hourly rate would change accordingly.

You should do your own math to find what *your* minimum hourly rate is at this moment and at this stage of your life and freelance career.

You are probably wondering how you could possibly come up with exact numbers of your personal or business expenses on a yearly basis right at this moment. You are right, you couldn't. But neither could I. The above numbers are estimated and are based on past experience. This formula will do a good enough job to help you figure out your minimum hourly rate. You can freely charge more depending on each project's specifics.

Don't get too hung up on it though. You cannot pinpoint an exact number for your minimum hourly rate but guess what—you don't need to do that anyway. If you commit *right now* to succeed on Upwork, there is a great chance that you will be charging at least a 20% higher rate in six months than you do now. So your minimum hourly rate then would be, even *should* be, different from your minimum hourly rate right now.

Just make sure you don't put a price of $10 per hour if you want to be hired at $30. In my own freelance career I've always set my rate to what I *would like* to earn, and as my knowledge and experience grew, I kept sliding it upwards. Besides, if more freelancers would stop setting rock-bottom rates, the playing field would be more level and everyone would get paid better rates.

To continue the example with the research I did in the sales & marketing category on Upwork, let's see what profile rate a starting marketer on Upwork can put.

First step is choosing your niche to prove yourself. Being a newbie freelancer without a proven track record on the site will make it impossible to land a high-paying consultancy contract, no matter how brilliant marketer you are. Clients will be more likely to award you a small-scale project to see how they work with you. They won't award you marketing planning for their business the moment they meet you.

Since social media marketing is on the rise, positioning yourself there might be a good idea to kick-start your freelance marketing career. Read all you can online—what's new in the industry, what's old, what's no longer working, what is effective, what gives quick results, what's recommended in the long run, what type of people are on which networks, what networks are good for what industries, what to avoid as it is not according to the rules of the specific social media network (Facebook, Twitter, LinkedIn, Pinterest, Instagram, Google+, and YouTube to name the major ones; they all have specific rules).

Educate yourself and specialize in one direction—e.g. lead generation through LinkedIn; or Facebook page management for fashion companies; or Twitter management for music artists; or integrated social media marketing communications for all types of small online businesses. These are just random examples. You decide what is it that you want to specialize in to prove yourself as a reliable freelancer on Upwork.

Start small—bid on projects for day-to-day activities management and when you are ready, make a step forward with SMM strategy planning to back-up your price requirements.

You can put whatever hourly rate you want on your profile—$5, $15, $50 ... but remember the results of your research. More importantly, remember who you are, what you do best, what you are worth and how much you want to get paid for your skills and expertise. Do not sell yourself short. Find your comfortable level to get started and stick to it.

A final note about your profile rate—it is not set in stone. As time passes and your completed projects grow, you will get more and better reviews which will add value to your freelance profile. Your services will be in higher demand which will allow you to broaden your horizons and get picky about clients and projects. And finally, your limited availability will enable you to increase your hourly rate to filter out the potential clients who are not ready to pay higher fees.

Rates for Fixed-Price Jobs

Learning to calculate your prices on fixed-price jobs will enable you to get paid for your skills and work, not for your time.

For example, I can get hired on Upwork to do a website review for $1,000, but I would probably not get hired for the same job for ten hours at an hourly rate of $100. *It's all about perception.*

In both cases I would get the same amount of money— but in one case the client will pay for my expertise. In the other case, the client will pay for my time and naturally, $100 per hour is a steep price to pay for a freelancer on Upwork.

You need to be able to calculate your prices on a project basis so that you have the flexibility to charge by the hour or by the project when your hourly rate is too high for the market.

There might be different reasons why you should prefer working on flat-rate projects. To name a few:

- You are a fast worker compared to the average freelancer and it is not lucrative to sell your time, rather you should sell your service.

- You spend more time offline while working and for that reason you cannot track your time with the Upwork online time tracker. You can only add offline time after the fact which may or may not be agreeable to your client if they hired you on an hourly basis project.

- You work as part of a team where everyone does their own tasks for the completion of a single project—and you get paid for the project, not for the task.

Whatever the reason, the single thing that matters the most is the completion of the fixed-price job on time, with the agreed quality and within budget.

If you are on the high end of the price range among your fellow freelancers, try to land fixed price jobs and not hourly gigs.

Here are a few questions to ask yourself when determining the flat rate you should charge for a specific project.

1) How many freelancers have applied for the flat-rate project job and what's their average rate?

This is purely for information. The preliminary announced budget and the active candidacies will give you an idea what type of freelancers have applied for the job. And the active interviews (or lack of such) will reveal what type of client you are about to deal with.

For instance, if there are few applicants and the average flat rate is above the announced budget, chances are the client has not estimated his costs well. He or she may have underestimated the complexity of the task, the skills or efforts needed to complete the fixed-price job on time; hence, the expected costs should be higher than anticipated and you can rest assured the client will not decline your application based on your higher price.

If the applicants' rates are around the estimated budget, but you estimate your flat rate higher than that, then you will have to match the price expectations or justify your higher rate with added value like faster delivery, higher quality, proven track record, etc.

2) What is your value proposition for the specific fixed-price job?

The answer to this question will help you craft your freelance proposal to stand apart from the crowd. For instance:

- If you have a proven track record in the client's niche, state it as your advantage. But don't just say, "I have completed X projects in your niche." Instead, focus on the fast delivery you will be able to provide them with because you have extensive knowledge in this niche as a result of X projects in the area successfully completed in the last Y months.

- If the fixed-price job is about data entry and you have incredibly fast and accurate typing skills, again state it as your advantage by focusing on the quick turn-around time and error-free file you will be able to provide them with as a result of the X successfully completed data entry projects in the last Y months for major companies like A, B, and C.

- If you have a wonderful voice and enunciation backed up with some radio ads, audio books, or podcast recordings in your portfolio, this might be just the tip you need to convince the client to pay you the higher rate you require for your services. Be sure not to focus on your wonderful voice and enunciation though. Instead, tell your prospective client your experience with audio books for children will enable you to perfectly read the mom's lines in his children's audio book without too many re-takes. This in turn would save him tons of time (and money) and will help him launch his new audio e-book on time for that big children event in his town.

All in all, clients often prefer paying a higher flat rate for the services of a well-established professional than less money for the inexperienced newbie freelancer's services. This is especially valid for one time fixed-price jobs.

3) How much time would you need to complete the flat-rate project?

The number of hours you'd need to complete the project multiplied by your minimum hourly rate should give you the *absolute* minimum flat rate you should charge for a specific fixed-price job. Let's take an example to explain why. Also, let's use $10 per hour for this example because it is easy to do the math.

If your minimum hourly rate is $10 per hour and you need ten hours to complete the fixed-price job, then the least bid you should place is $100 (ten hours x $10 per hour).

I often overstate the flat rate per project by 20-30% for a couple of main reasons:

- When I overstate the price, I am flexible enough to make additional edits if the client requests any, without asking for additional budget. Thanks to this little gesture, the client would see me as a freelancer on whom they can rely in a crisis or when a quick edit is required. Hence, it could potentially bring me more work and turn this client into a repeat one.

- With the markup of 20-30% I am flexible to make discounts if the competition for the job boils down to price. It happens rarely, but sometimes a few very good freelancers compete for the same job. They all bring added value. They all have great competitive advantages. They are all so great and good and suitable for the position that the client is left with no choice but to choose the least expensive.

So, in the context of the above example, if my hourly rate were $10 and I needed ten hours to complete the project, I would bid $120-$130.

And remember, when working on fixed-price jobs, you sell your skills and services, and not your time. Don't compete on price, but add value for your client. Provide them with great experience and they will choose you over the competition that offered low price but didn't make them feel special.

How Much Money Can You Make?

"How much money can I make as a freelancer on Upwork?" is one of the most asked questions I get in my mailbox by fellow freelancers who are just starting their freelance practice. The simple answer is "it depends on your skills and your niche of expertise."

I cannot answer this question with an exact number because when you commit to succeed as a freelancer, unlimited opportunities lie before you. **You can make as little as you want or as much as you want**—it totally depends on how much you want to work, how good you are at what you do, what's the demand of your skills, and how you price your services. Know what you are worth and you can make exactly so much as you want and deserve.

A lot of freelancers who come from low socioeconomic countries like India, Pakistan, the Philippines, and even Eastern European countries, think it's impossible to make a good living as a freelancer. (I am from one of these countries, I should know!) They are used to getting paid low wages and think it's normal to be so when they are freelancers, too.

In reality, no matter where you live, you *can and should* sell your services for what they are worth. After all, that's why you became a freelancer—to put yourselves out there and to work on a world-class level. To do so, you should break free from the assumption you can or cannot make more money compared to what you used to make as an employee.

You simply should start thinking about making more money, period. Don't compare—think big in terms of making more money per hour or per project. Only if you stop comparing your income to your last day job, should you be able to ditch the forty-hour work week and start working smarter, not harder.

Think what you want to make and plan how to get there.

I know speaking "in theory" isn't convincing, nor all that useful, so let me put it into perspective.

I will give you examples how much money a marketing consultant and a graphic designer can make, working as a freelancer on Upwork, from what I have seen in my experience so far.

Making a living as a graphic designer.

As a potential graphic designer, researching their competition on Upwork, you will see there are designers willing to work for as little as $5 or $10 per hour.

I have hardly ever found a good designer working at this wage. Usually those are people who have mediocre (at best) designer's skills. They have little to no feeling for color matching or aesthetics. They have little to no knowledge about user experience. Those freelancers are able to work with designer's programs like Photoshop, Illustrator, and alike but that's about all they can do.

Tell them *exactly* what you want—maybe they'll get it right. I am sorry I have to break this to you, but if you are one of those designers, unless you drastically improve your skills, that's about all the money you can make as a freelance graphic designer.

If you are a true artist though, and for whatever reason you charge as little as five or ten bucks per hour, stop right now. Lean back and think about what you want.

As I mentioned before, good clients know they will get what they pay for. If you have extraordinary skills, why compete on price with those who lack them? If you charge pennies for great work, you will always find yourself working with unappreciative clients who are after the quick deal, not after the long-term relationship with a true artist like yourself.

Maybe someone at some point told you to cut your prices in order to land designing jobs. That's not entirely true. Working for less money than you deserve in the beginning of your career may be a sound tactic to land a few projects to get started, but **bidding under the competition for the sake of price is *never* a good idea.**

When you charge $5-10 per hour for designing skills, you put yourself in front of all those clients who don't care about quality—they have costs as their highest priority.

You may land a job with them, but you will never get to land a job with a quality client who would appreciate you for your artist skills.

If you are a good designer, you can start charging anywhere between $25 and $50 right away. If you are a great designer, with a little help from a marketing professional, you can position yourself right and start charging top dollar for your work from day one.

As your experience as a freelancer grows, you can start taking only fixed-price jobs with clear terms of collaboration where your hourly rate could amount to $75, even $100+ per hour.

The situation is similar when making a living as a freelance marketing consultant.

There are "marketing gurus" available on Upwork for as little as $7 per hour. Unfortunately, I was one of them when I was starting in the beginning of 2010 but in my defense, I didn't know better.

Coming from a low socioeconomic country where the minimum hourly pay rate was less than a dollar at the time, charging $7 per hour was a huge success on my behalf, or so I thought.

In hindsight, charging such low rates may have delayed my freelance success. Sure, it helped me land projects, but the clients I was attracting were not paying well. Even worse, a high-paying client would have never taken me seriously with such a low hourly rate. Because I charged so little, they would have expected my work not to be good and simply moved on.

You can find a marketing expert on Upwork for an hourly rate between $7 and $100+.

Not surprisingly, the majority of marketing experts who charge $7-$10 per hour are not very knowledgeable. They know some SEO, they may be able to handle your blog scheduling, browse your Google analytics data, assist you in various marketing tasks like web research, book and email formatting, etc. They have heard this is all in the marketing domain of any business so they called themselves marketing experts.

You can find decent freelancers for $7 to $10 per hour, but sooner or later they all increase their rates when they realize they are worth much more and can get paid way more for their services.

The freelance marketers who work for years at $7-10 per hour are probably good workers who cannot work on their own and are happy with the place they are at. Which is cool since everybody has the right to choose what to do and how to do it.

If you are a freelance marketer who has greater plans for themselves (and if you are asking me how much money you can make—I suppose you do!), I will tell you the same thing I told the designers above—stop charging pennies and think about what you want.

If you are good with following instructions, work well on a daily basis when a clear objective and tasks are defined, but you lack the experience and expertise to plan on a strategic level or manage your own team—then you can start by charging anywhere between $10 and $20 per hour on Upwork.

If you are smart and willing to learn and improve, you can grow, too—you don't have to stay at the same level forever and your wage will grow along with your experience and skills.

If you can think independently though and help clients with strategy planning, then you can charge more.

Rates run from $20 to $50 per hour for social media marketing planning, through $75 per hour for team training and management, to $100+ per hour for consulting, marketing project management and coaching. The latter is harder to be found on Upwork—working directly with clients is a better option.

As your experience as a freelance marketing consultant grows, you will be better at estimating the time and effort needed to complete a task. So you will be able to take more fixed-price jobs and calculate your prices in such a way that your hourly rate would amount at $50 or $100 per hour even if the gig is not as high level as coaching but more along the lines of integrated marketing planning or even content writing for marketing purposes.

As discussed before, your price depends on many factors.

To name a few, the complexity of the task at hand, your experience and skill level, how busy you are, turnaround time, as well as how well known and referable you are, and so on.

And let's not forget when working as a freelancer, you have the freedom to decide how much you want to work. Your income is proportional not only to your hourly wage but to the amount of working hours you put in.

If you work twenty hours per week at $25 per hour, you'll make $500 per week before taxes.

If you work forty hours per week at $25 per hour, you'll make $1,000 per week before taxes.

If you work twenty hours per week at $50 per hour, you'll make again $1,000 per week before taxes.

And if you choose to work twenty hours per week and can land only high-paying gigs at $100 per hour, your income would amount to $2,000 per week before taxes.

You can of course work on some projects at $25 and others at $50. It all depends on the project and complexity of work. Just make sure you don't accept a project below your minimum hourly rate.

All of these scenarios are possible—it all depends on what you want and what you are capable of. As you can see, how much money you make as a freelancer is very subjective.

If there is one takeaway here, it would be that anything and everything is possible. It really is a matter of goal setting, planning, and sticking to the plan afterwards. It is all in your hands and nobody else's.

Homework to Position Yourself on the Market

- Research your competition on Upwork and find the right spot for yourself on the market in terms of offered skills, client's benefits, and price range.

- Decide what niche you'll specialize in to make a name for yourself on the freelance job board.

- Find your minimum hourly wage and put it on your profile.

- As an exercise, browse some projects that interest you and practice your flat rate calculating skills.

- Pitch a friend of yours as if they were the client looking for a freelancer for the specific project, and then ask for their feedback on how well you did.

- Do this for five more projects taking into account new feedback you received from your pretend-clients each time.

STEP 5: PICK THE RIGHT PROJECTS AND CLIENTS

Once you know where you want to position yourself on the market, you should stay away from some clients— those who don't respect you as a professional, who don't pay fair rates, who don't pay at all, who lack communication skills, and so on.

I know it may sound strange to you now. "Wait, what? Pick clients? Is she crazy? I need to put food on the table. How can I be picky about paying work and clients?!"

Been there, done that. There were a few times when I was not picky and started working with a couple of clients whom I didn't like and didn't want to work with. In the end, I've regretted entering a contract with them. *It's never too early to be picky.*

Choosing your clients wisely early on will help you position yourself on Upwork and attract the right crowd—the good clients who respect you and are willing to pay top dollar for your skills and expertise.

Clients to Avoid

Not all clients are created equal. You should definitely avoid some, so take the time to learn how to recognize them.

Let's call them bad clients, but not because they are bad people or anything. They are just those clients who are more likely to cause trouble and disappointment in the long run rather than help you grow personally and professionally.

The Bargainer

Potentially bad clients who fall in this category always try to cut your pay rate.

Many people are used to bargaining and look for the best price for products, services, etc. When it comes to freelancing, it's a bit different (or at least it *should* be). Being a freelancer, you are not just selling your time or skills. You are adding value. Like I mentioned before, your client is paying not for the hour you need to complete the job; they are paying for your expertise, for the years you needed to acquire those skills to do the job in an hour.

If a client persistently tries to cut your rates, most likely they won't be happy with your work in the end. Not for some other reason, but because they entered the contract with the single thought, "I am paying too much for this!"

A very important distinction you need to make is between clients who negotiate and clients who bargain.

If a client has a certain budget to fit in and your price quote for the project is out of that budget, you can negotiate your rate by decreasing the scope of activities, increasing the turn-around time, getting paid in advance in full, adding milestone payments as opposed to one big payout, or something else to compensate the decreased rate.

Clients who bargain don't care about all of the above; they simply want to give you less money than you asked for, for no good reason.

Good clients appreciate the value. I know I have said it already, several times, but so many starting freelancers don't realize this early enough that I simply feel obliged to reiterate it once more—good clients hire you for the benefits they will gain from your skills, experience, and expertise. They don't think about the price—they think about the value for that price. So as long as you have a reasonable pricing strategy and know how much you're worth, you should stay away from bad clients who try to bargain at any cost and every time.

The Micromanager

As a freelancer, you are no longer an office employee. You are an independent and professional consultant who has their own working style and habits. You have the freedom to plan your time and work as you please. Here are a few things that bad clients want (one at a time or all at once):

- monitor your work constantly

- demand that you are available on Skype during working hours

- require multiple e-mails, updates, and reports every day, several times per day

- expect accountability for every minute spent working on their project

These clients have trust issues. They have a hard time believing you actually know what you're doing. They don't think you'll do your job on time and with the agreed quality, unless they are pushing you and standing over your shoulder. They think they know better and you just need to do what they tell you.

I would suggest staying away from such clients. They call for trouble because they don't appreciate your experience and professionalism. Even worse, they probably think you don't really have what it takes to do the job. They often feel you might get it right but only if you strictly follow their instructions, regardless if they are experts in your field.

The Unpleasable

Clients who don't really know what they want are impossible to please. Stay away from them.

Never take upon contracts with no clear goals and expected results. As a freelancer, you go through interviews not only so the client to get to know you. Freelance interviews are also to help *you*, the freelancer, decide if you want to work on certain projects and with certain clients.

If you exchange a couple of e-mails and even meet with them on Skype but still do not have a clear idea about the project, its time frame, expected results and your role in it, the client probably doesn't really know what they want and the outcome won't be satisfactory to them.

I have seen many freelancers ignore the signs and enter a contract with such clients even though they suspected something was off. I have even done it myself. Twice. Nothing fatal will happen if you do, too. You will just waste some time, feel frustrated for a while, and eventually learn your lesson that such clients are to be avoided. The next time you encounter such a client, it's your choice whether to learn your lesson the hard way or learn from my mistakes and move on.

Communication is one of the most important things for a successful freelancer-client relationship. Never compromise with it. Always work with clients who know what they want and have a clear idea about the end game, the expected results, as well as the freelancer's responsibilities.

It's okay to help a client find out what they need and want—those you keep because they will be loyal to you for life if you can help them figure out what they want *and* deliver it to them. But the clients who don't know what they want and are not capable of following your lead to learn, those are clients you should leave and never look back.

The Indecisive

Indecisive clients can be very bad for you, too. Those are the clients who are not able to make up their mind. Does the following sound familiar?

"Is this the right thing to do? Is this the right time to do it? Am I paying too much? Will you really do a good job? Maybe I should think about it a little more—yes, I know I've been thinking about it for a week now and we've met twice already but ... Is this the right thing to do? Is this the right time to do it? Will I get my return on investment?"

The client is obviously hesitant to commit. They may be just indecisive. Or they may be fishing for information so they can implement your idea without you. Whatever the case, you are better off without them. You want clients who are willing and eager to work with you—not because you want to but because they see how much you can help them move forward.

The Question-Dodger

The way clients react to freelancers' questions speaks a lot about their integrity as clients. If a prospect ignores your questions about the project and your future collaboration, you'd better move on. Let me explain why.

I understand clients have busy schedules. What saddens me is that clients often don't realize that freelancers do, too. It happens sometimes that I ask questions related to their business, niche, project goals, duration, etc. and I get a short reply like, "Find me on Skype to discuss."

First, I won't waste my time discussing a project I don't want to be involved in. And if the client doesn't address my questions, I won't know if I am or am not interested in it. I prefer to read their answers on my own time and decide if I want to speak further. Besides, having the answers in writing allows for a record of communication for future reference, if need be.

Second, I don't go to a freelance interview (or any Skype meeting for that matter) without any preparation whatsoever. And if the client doesn't address my questions, I have no idea who they are, what they do, or what they want and expect.

Third, I don't appreciate the attitude and notion that I should get running toward the client the moment I hear back from them with their Skype ID and no further details about my questions, time, and date for a possible meeting, etc. This implies they expect me to be on Skype all day looking for them or worse, waiting for them to come so we can further discuss.

There's no way any of this can happen. I value my time too much and there are too many good clients out there to waste my time with bad ones. I advise you to do the same. **When you encounter a client who ignores your questions—don't think twice, just move on.**

The One Who Doesn't Like Escrow

If you take upon fixed-price jobs on Upwork, always make sure the client has awarded the project to you and placed funds in escrow before starting the project.

Depending on the project scale and your preferences, you can have a single-milestone contract or break it in several milestones. In any case, be sure the milestones are funded and the client's money is placed safely in Escrow.

If you encounter a client who refuses and says they won't pay anything upfront under no circumstances (some clients mistakenly think funding milestones through Escrow is the same as upfront payment), you may have a bad client. Chances are you'll do your job and then they won't pay at all with the lame excuse "you didn't do what I asked" and that's the end of it.

Only if the client funds a milestone on Upwork, are you guaranteed to get paid after delivery. It's that simple. Don't make exceptions.

The One Who Likes Free Work

You may encounter the occasional client on Upwork who asks for a sample to determine the quality of work. That's fine—they don't know you, it's okay to ask for samples. The trouble starts when they ask for a sample that you do *especially* for them, and for free.

Having a trial assignment before committing to the long term is a good idea for both clients and freelancers. But in no universe is it okay to have that trial assignment free of charge. If you have a prospective client asking you to work for free, move on—you shouldn't waste your time and energy on people who don't respect your time and skills.

The One You Just Don't Like

Trust your gut—if you dislike your future client or their project, decline right away.

This doesn't have much to do with good or bad clients. It is more about your personal experience, intuition, and preferences. If you don't like the product which you need to market, to write about, to design a package for, whatever else you do—then probably your work won't be good either.

If the potential client irritates you in some way (condescending attitude, rudeness, lack of respect, poor communication skills, inability to express their thoughts, etc.), there's a pretty good chance you won't be able to do successful business with them. This will ultimately worsen the end result of the collaboration, and lead only to frustration and, quite possibly, negative feedback on your résumé.

Start Choosing Your Clients as Early as Possible

For many, it may seem strange that I am suggesting you to be picky about clients. For professionals who just start their freelance careers, the beginning is hard and every single project counts and is welcome. **However, I urge you to think in perspective**.

If you take on a low-paying, boring, unsatisfying, whatever-else-bad-thing-you-could-think-of   project right now, you risk being stuck with it for months. Don't fall in the trap of working with a bad client who is worse than the boss you had on the last office job you tried so hard to escape from.

Once you get the ball rolling and have a few successful projects on Upwork, you will have the freedom to choose with whom to work and on what projects. Then it's a matter of principle to watch out for bad clients and not deal with them at all.

After all, you are a freelancer so you can feel good about yourself, your work, and your life—don't forget that, ever!

Get to Know the Client through Their Job Post

Your success as a freelancer is not about the number of projects you apply to. It's about the type of projects you apply to. You can learn a great deal about your future client from their profile and from the way they constructed their job post.

I will walk you through the process of choosing your projects. For illustrative purposes, I will include a few screenshots from random job posts on Upwork. Note that I am in no way affiliated with any of the job posts used in this section.

Here are a few factors you should take into account when deciding whether a client and a job post are worth your time and effort to apply.

Client Registration

Look when the freelance client registered on Upwork. If they are a long-time member of the website, most probably they also have a verified payment method as well as having spent a reasonable amount of money on the platform. If you calculate the ratio between money spent and time since registration, you will find out how active the client is in reality.

For instance, a better freelance client is the one who has spent $20,000 during the last six months than the client who has spent $5,000 for the last two years. The latter obviously hires very low-paid workers or doesn't use the platform as often.

Be aware though that the time of registration out of context may or may not mean anything. See the screenshot below:

About the Client

New to oDesk

United States
Austin 02:25 PM

3 JOBS POSTED
0% Hire Rate, 1 Open Job

Member Since: Nov 29, 2013

This is a freelance client with a verified payment method who registered a few of years ago but has zero spending for the moment. This doesn't make them a bad client, but combined with other factors, this could give you plenty of information about the type of client you are about to deal with.

Payment Method

Check if your prospective client's payment method is verified.

Clients with verified payment method display a green tick symbol ( ) in the client's information section. Those without a verified payment method say so:

About the Client

Payment Method Not Verified (?)

Again, if they are registered for a long time, most probably they do have a verified payment method.

If the freelance client is newly registered and their status is "payment method verified" or "payment method verification in progress," this usually means the client is serious about hiring a contractor through the platform.

If the freelance client is newly registered and has a status "payment method not verified," it does not necessarily mean they are not a serious client, but it certainly means they are less serious and won't bother verifying their payment method before actually finding the right fit for their project.

If the freelance client registered a long time ago (as in a few months or more) and still doesn't have a verified payment method—I wouldn't bother applying, unless the job post is extremely interesting and suitable to my interests and needs at the moment.

Published Jobs / Hired Freelancers Ratio

Another factor to consider when deciding about a potential client is their ratio of published job posts and hired freelancers.

As you most probably know by now, there are a lot of freelancers from countries with low socioeconomic standards who are willing to work for very little to no money per hour. Sometimes, it is very hard to filter low-quality workers and find suitable candidates if the client needs specialized quality work done. Having said this, here's how you can use the ratio number of posts / hired contractors for each client.

The lower the ratio, the better the client.

If the potential client has published many job posts (including republished ones), but has hired just a handful of freelancers—then, this client would be more likely to pay a higher pay rate as long as you have a proven track record on or off the freelance job board and more importantly, you are a good specialist in your field.

If the potential freelance client has hired someone for every single job post they have published, most probably that client is looking for cheap labor and wouldn't care for quality. Move on.

Let's see a random job post on Upwork as an example. This is a client who has good ratio of job posts to hires but doesn't look like a good prospect to me.

About the Client

★★★★★ (5.00) 15 reviews

United States
Unionville 02:13 PM

59 Jobs Posted
43% Hire Rate, 2 Open Jobs

$5,069 Total Spent
28 Hires, 4 Active

$1.62/hr Avg Hourly Rate Paid
2,017 Hours

Member Since Mar 27, 2011

This freelance client has posted 59 jobs and has hired only twenty-eight people at a 43% hire rate. However, I wouldn't bother applying as this client has a proven track record of low paying preferences—an average hourly rate of $1.62.

To double-check this, I would go and see their history of contracts on the same page where one can find information about past contracts, at what rates, and for how many hours (if an hourly job), etc.

I might have given this client the benefit of the doubt, if most of their projects were fixed price and the extremely low average hourly rate of past hires was a result of a couple of very old projects. However, it's evident in this client's work history that he or she is in the habit of paying pennies for all kinds of work. No good client on Upwork would even think of making someone work for such low rates, no matter the circumstances. It is up to you if you want to apply. I would move on as it would take a lot of effort on my part to make the client change their behavior and start valuing (and paying for) skills and competencies.

Client's Feedback

If the freelance client is newly registered, obviously he or she won't have any feedback yet. You can draw conclusions if they have open projects for a few months, at least. If they have freelancers working with them on a regular basis for long periods of time, chances are this is a good client.

If the client has feedback and ratings, pay attention what projects they are for—hourly or fixed price, long-term or short-term, etc. A client may be a great partner for hourly projects and not so much on fixed-price jobs.

For example, if all freelancers have left a certain client five-star feedback for fixed-price jobs, this means the specific client probably holds their end of the contract—no scope creep or withheld payments (as long as you do your job, of course).

However, you might encounter a client who has impeccable feedback for hourly paid projects and average or poor feedback for fixed-price jobs. This might mean that the client is a prompt payer as long as you record diligently your work activities, but he is a problematic client for fixed-price jobs because he adds tasks to the overall project without adjusting the price quote, which results in scope creep or withheld payments. In this case, you might be better off working by the hour with them and staying away from their fixed-price projects.

Another example I'd like to give is with short vs long-term contracts. It is possible that the freelance client has excellent reviews for short-term jobs but bad feedback on long-term ones because he or she fails to communicate well, or is too controlling, or something else. So this client would be a good fit if you are applying to a quick job but not for a one-year contract.

Let's see a real-life example of how to extract information about clients from their feedback.

This freelance client has hired different contractors for the same types of jobs—transcription and translation in different languages. Hourly rates are not available, but by doing the math on fixed-price jobs for transcription, it would amount to $0.69 to $0.93 per audio minute, which is about the average going rate on Upwork for this type of work. We don't have enough data to determine the hourly rates for the translation contracts, but on a deeper look, you can see that the profile rates of the hired freelancers vary from $15 to $25 per hour, which is again an average rate for translation on Upwork. Furthermore, this client sticks with the same freelancers—he or she has hired many of them on multiple contracts. So my educated guess about this client would be twofold.

This freelance client knows the price depends on how rare a certain language is, for translation jobs, or how urgent the task is, for transcription jobs. As a result, he or she is willing to pay for quality or quick turnaround time. Once the client finds a reliable freelancer who does their job well and on time, he or she is willing to stick with them and hire them on multiple occasions. This client appreciates a good relationship with freelancers.

When I browsed the full work history of the client, I saw there was not a single project that paid by the hour, and their feedback and reviews were great for almost all contracts—one time or repeat. This is definitely a good client. If I were interested and suitable, I would apply to this job post.

Applicants and Interviews

When looking at possible projects, you don't have information about the freelancers who have applied to the job post. Yet how many people have applied is visible, as well as if there are any active interviews.

Depending on the active interviews (or lack of such), you will know the job post's urgency. If it is published a day ago and already shows ten interviews, this means the freelance client is in a hurry to hire someone. If the job post is published for days and there are still no active interviews, this means the freelance client is taking their time to filter candidates and gather resumes. Quality for the latter is much more important than finding someone and soon.

If you have a Plus account (see Appendix 2: URL References), you will also see the minimum, average, and maximum bid for the specific project, which may or may not be necessarily beneficial.

If you employ the tactics outlined in this book, you will most probably focus on the value you bring to the table by offering a bid that reflects that, regardless what your competition does.

Information in the Job Post

Consider how much information the job post offers. Is it super-short or does it provide enough details about the project? Does it offer information on the company's background? Does it list only requirements for the freelancer or also responsibilities that go with the job and project details?

Choose well-written and clear job posts as those are usually written by clients with good communication skills. I bet you've seen job posts like this one:

The problem with this ad is that it gives no information whatsoever about the client, about the project, or what preliminary information will be given, if any (e.g. target audience profile, extensive research about their problems and needs, etc.), what your role would be (just polishing the draft based on the target audience profile and preliminary information, or also research and copywriting) or details about the niche, the type of content and its purpose in general. Not to mention that $20 budget is quite possibly low for such a project.

Allow me to provide a quick note about project budgets and why you shouldn't immediately dismiss someone for what you deem a "ridiculously low budget."

It's necessary to put a number in the budget field when posting a job, but some clients are not sure what the appropriate amount of money is for the work they need done. As a result, they place the minimum budget of five dollars even though they are prepared to pay hundreds or thousands of dollars to the right freelancer. However, those clients usually state in their job post that they are not certain about the appropriate budget for the task at hand.

Here are a few pointers on what a good job post contains and how a good client would construct their post when searching for a freelancer:

- **Clear and informative title**—for example, if the client is looking for "a translator," it doesn't really say what languages or what type of content is to be translated. However, a title "English-Spanish Translator wanted for daily blog posts" tells not only the required languages but also the workload (daily blog posts means daily work)

- **Business introduction**—if the client has included a brief introduction of their business, they are probably looking for a freelancer with whom to work long term. If they have included their website in the job post, they are probably testing you to see if you will make the extra effort to check out their website before writing your proposal. A bad client will never bother to do this. Only a good client will put so much thought into their job post.

- **Available information about the job**—the more details the client has included, the better prospect he or she is. Such details that might be expected are weekly workload, estimated project duration, responsibilities, time table, budget, existing work flow and work process, and so on. All of these details can be easily covered in a 500-word job post.

- **Specific questions asked**—good clients most often filter suitable candidates as early as their job post. The easiest way to do that is by asking specific questions that only a suitable candidate would be able to answer.

Note that if a job post does not have all of the above, this does not necessarily mean the client is bad. However the more of those the job post contains, the better the client is. Job posts which contain nothing of the described are more likely to waste your time.

Make it a habit to look at every job post from the prism of all these elements of what constitutes a good client. Look at the post title, look at the information available, are there questions, and so on. Do this enough times and on a regular basis, and you will easily be able to learn more about your prospect within two minutes of opening their job post.

Homework to Start Picking the Right Clients

- Take all that I shared about bad clients and create a checklist. <u>Here's a checklist I give away to my community</u> (see Appendix 2: URL References)—you can use it but don't be afraid to add other red flags noticed during the course of your practice. Always make sure your prospects fit your requirements for a good client.

- Open Upwork and start browsing the available job posts in your niche.

- Pick a job post to analyze in order to learn more about the client who posted it.

- Do this for five more job posts—by the time you are finished, you will learn how to recognize good and bad clients from their job posts before even speaking to them.

STEP 6: MASTER THE ART OF PROPOSAL WRITING

In my freelance career, I've been a team manager multiple times and hired many freelance contractors. So I speak from experience on both sides of the fence—I have written many proposals, and I've read my fair share too.

It makes a bad first impression if you apply to all jobs with a recycled freelance cover letter. Clients *know* if you do so as the information in the letter often appears irrelevant. What's even worse, you demonstrate lack of attention to detail or interest in general.

I have hired freelancers through Upwork on behalf of clients—social media marketers, SEO experts, virtual assistants, transcribers, writers, designers, and programmers, and in all these areas the percentage of recycled proposals was fairly high, anywhere between 75-90%. So I know whatever your profession, writing a proposal customized specifically for the project you apply to, will instantly differentiate you from the competition.

Here are some dos and don'ts that will help you write great proposals and land more projects on Upwork.

Follow Instructions

It's no coincidence many job posts on Upwork ask to start a cover letter with a code word of some kind. The sole purpose is to filter out freelancers who apply with recycled cover letters and don't bother even reading the project description when applying.

Often the requirement is to *start* the letter with the code word because it is visible to the client before they even open the full proposal. They can easily decline the application without reading because it didn't start with the code word. So read carefully and follow the instructions to stay in the race.

Answer All Questions

Often clients want to save time and interview only a couple of good freelancers most suitable for the job. These clients give very detailed requirements in their job posts and include specific questions. Don't say you'll answer the questions during the interview as you may not make it to that stage.

Make sure to address all questions asked by the client in your proposal. What I usually do is I open a new Word document and then copy and paste the questions and sections that need addressing. I write my answers in between the lines to make sure I answer all their questions. I then read it from start to end and cross off redundancies. I read once more to proofread my proposal and to make sure it reads smoothly and includes both the questions and my answers accordingly.

Make your answers detailed, on topic, and to the point. Emphasize your characteristics, qualifications, and qualities that are required and useful *specifically* for the project. Explain how these characteristics will help the client achieve their goal. This is the only way you will stand apart from the crowd and will have a chance to reach the interview stage with the client.

Ask Questions

Answering all questions from the job post may be enough for you to go to an interview. However, if you ask some questions of your own in your proposal, it will show the client you are a serious candidate.

Many freelancers think of questions to ask but leave them for the interview. Truth be told, you may or may not reach the interview stage. Asking questions as early as your proposal differentiates you from the competition and shows you have spent some time thinking about the project. You have envisioned your role and actively thought what you might need to carry it out. If your questions are good and on topic, the interview will be yours.

Demonstrate Your Skills

In my experience, it's good to provide the client an idea specifically related to the project in question. For example, let's say you apply for a SMM position. The client is looking for someone to create a SMM strategy for their LinkedIn (LI) company page and group. Take the time to look through both the page and the group and give them an idea how to improve their presence on LinkedIn.

Such an idea could be the suggestion to add group rules to the LI group. This way they will improve the overall member experience and moderation workflow because it will be clear what rules apply to their group.

Another idea could be to bring variety in the updates they share on their company page (one day a link to their new blog post, the next day a link to one of their videos on YouTube, then a text update with a quote for inspiration, etc.) Explain that bringing variety in their page updates will keep the community engaged and will create expectancy in their audience for the information being shared and for the usefulness of the page in general.

These suggestions are good enough to show your experience and expertise in SMM on LinkedIn. Also, they reveal plenty about your way of thinking as a social media marketer. Just be careful not to go into too much detail or you risk giving the idea away so someone else could implement it without you. Your suggestions should provoke the client's interest toward you, nothing more.

Mind Your Grammar and Spelling

If English is not your mother tongue, don't worry— nobody will hold you responsible. However, punctuation, spelling, and proper grammar could differentiate you.

Don't abbreviate. I know how easy and quickly it is to write "smth" instead of "something," or "ppl" instead of "people," or "pls" instead of "please" ... Don't do it.

If you abbreviate when applying to a project, you risk being misunderstood or not understood at all. Or worse, those abbreviations communicate, "I am so busy that I cannot write the whole word," or "You're not worthy of my time at this stage so I won't waste it in writing all words in full."

You never know who is reading your cover letter and how they will perceive abbreviations.

Always recheck your proposal before hitting the send button. Read it twice—the second time focus *only* on punctuation, spelling, and grammar as opposed to the content focus of the earlier round of editing.

Use Simple Sentences

Forget about using a lot of words without saying anything. Stay on topic. Give structure to your thoughts and explain ideas in a few words.

All of this speaks for the ability to do your job on time and according to the preliminary agreement. Your clients will be more likely to award their project to you if persuaded with arguments and not with small talk. Ask a writer-friend to go through your cover letter and give feedback for strong and weak points in your draft. Edit where needed. If you have the budget, you can hire a professional editor to help on a regular basis.

Don't be one of those freelancers who tell the story of their lives in their proposals. No client will look through the fifty-three links provided to see how much work you have done before.

Instead, focus on the project specifics and share only those items from your portfolio which are highly relevant to the job post at hand. Share *a few* examples.

Simply state more examples are available in your portfolio. Encourage the client to ask for more by telling them you have vast experience in your niche and can give them more examples on request. If you pick two or three samples which are highly relevant to the project, clients will rarely, if ever ask you for more work samples.

Samples of Proposals

To show how to put all of the above into practice, I will share a few good and bad real-life examples. Here is a job post I wrote for a client some time ago when looking for a social media marketing specialist.

> **SMM expert needed - financial background required - 4**
>
> Hourly Job, Part Time, More than 6 months
> Hourly Rate: $5.00 - $20.00 per hour
>
> We are looking for a social media marketing enthusiast to help us build our network of connections and manage daily activities online through social networks like Facebook, Twitter, LinkedIn, and YouTube. Google+ is an option, too in the long term. The strategic plan of SMM is already developed.
>
> Our websites are in the financial industry – so knowledge about how Financial Advisors think

and what their challenges are is essential and required.

***Please, read the job post carefully and include in your cover letter ONLY your answers to the questions asked - nothing more, thank you. ***

Please, apply for the job only if you are serious and looking for long term relationship. You need to cover all the requirements. Be prepared for a Skype interview prior to hiring.

To filter all automatic responses, please start your reply with the phrase: "financial advisor." Here are the questions to answer in your cover letter:

1. Tell us in a few sentences why you are a good fit for this project and how you can help us build a strong following on the web.

2. Tell us in details what is your financial background and/or experience in relation to financial advisors needs and specifics?

3. Give us an example of 3 tactics you employ to increase engagement of the audience on a company FB page.

4. Give us as example 3 FB pages you are particularly proud of - ONLY 3, the ones you are most proud of!!!

5. Give us an example of 3 tactics you employ to increase the friends and followers engagement on a company twitter profile

6. What is your experience with LinkedIn - what primarily you have been using it for so far?

7. What is your experience on YouTube and how do you decide the course of action there?

And here are the requirements we had included in the job post:

Job Requirements - core skills:

1. Excellent English (verbal and written)

2. Knowledge about how Financial Advisors think and what their challenges are

3. experienced in SMM

4. responsible and honest

5. organized and sensitive to deadlines

6. initiative and creative – SMM is all about engagement

7. capable of following instructions, keeping deadlines and submitting reports in timely manner

8. a team player

Minimum Required Experience:

- English Level 5

- Feedback score of at least 4.5

- Individual contractors ONLY

- Passed test: U.S. English Basic Skills Test & Social Media Marketing Test

Skills Required

Facebook Marketing, Social Media Marketing, Twitter Marketing, YouTube Marketing

Job additional information and Preferred Qualifications

Freelancer Type: Freelancers Only
Feedback Score: At least 4.50
Hourly Rate: $5.00/hr - $20.00/hr
English Level: Fluent - Has complete command of this language with perfect grammar

I reposted this job post four times before I finally found a freelancer who fit all my requirements. I received over 100 proposals, 90% of which were recycled and not customized in any way.

Here are a few examples of cover letters I received for this job post.

A VERY Bad Proposal

Hello,
I am [name of contractor] of expert of Social

Media Marketing.
I have very good experiences SMM Of Odesk
with portfolio. , I always understand Client job
Description and follow my clients instruction
about their project to makethem happy. I
respect My job, Odesk policy, client
requirement & delivery client work report in
time.
kind Regards
[name again]

This cover letter is so short that it brings no information whatsoever. Not to mention the bad punctuation, spelling, and grammar, while the job post clearly states fluency in English with perfect grammar is required. Saying you can follow instructions and then failing to follow the instructions of the job post doesn't do you any favors. Read carefully and apply accordingly—that is a key.

A Bad Proposal

Sir,
   Thank you very much post your project. I am
very much interested on
your project.
From my Experience and Expertise I believe and
very confident that I
will be able to handle your project efficiently
and effectively. I am
able to do 20-30 ads post an hour.
I have Experience SEO,SMM,SEM,Facebook fan
page, Face book likes,

Advertising, linkbilding,posting, youtub.Twitter,
I can do use
HTML,XHTML,CSS,for fan page, I know how to
get much traffic. I have
Confident that I will be able to incising your web
site page rank.
I have experience of face book and twitter,
1. Key-word research
2. Facebook posting
3.facebook markating
4.Social book marking,
5. Article submission
6, twitter followers
7. Blog comment
8. Social media markating.
9. Forum posting,
10. Article spinning
11.RSS
12. Directory Submission.
13.Web2.0 marketing
I am quite confident that I will be able to get
your work done within
the given time your requirements conclude.
Sincerely
[name of contractor]

First off, I never indicated I am a sir in the job post.
Assuming I am is rude and speaks of lack of experience
in working in an online environment. Also, as you can
see, not only is this cover letter a recycled one, this
freelancer was not even interested in the job we had to
offer. We were looking for a marketer to help us build
our network of connections and manage daily activities

online through social networks, while this applicant wanted to help us with outdated (and quite possibly black-hat) link building techniques. They had specialties, for the lack of a better word, in a totally different area than the one we were interested in. Not to mention the poor command of English he demonstrated which was a deal breaker on its own.

An Obviously Recycled Proposal

Hi,

I possess 4+ years of extensive expertise in social media marketing and am expert in working on platforms like FB, Gplus, Pinterest, Twitter, LinkedIn etc.

Just want to give you a quick background about myself, I am post graduated in computer application from a well reputed university, experienced in Internet Marketing and Social Media services working from the past 4+ years!!

Please find the attached portfolio, resume and profile detail!

Why you should hire me:

(1) I possess 4+ years of extensive experience in the social media target niche
(2) Honest, hard worker and strong believer in ROI!!
(3) I have a work load of 5 hours from other

project at this time and I can work on your project in a more focussed way.

(4) Hootsuite Certified Consultant

(5) For a social media plan, My favourite method is [here he included a detailed explanation and a step-by-step model how he goes about building a social media strategy for his clients.]

One of my strengths is my ability to identify content which will resonate with the audience and encourage interaction and sharing.
My fee is my hourly rate and includes daily Social Media management (posting content, interaction with other pages/profiles etc liking/commenting/retweeting where appropriate and beneficial for your brand, responding to comments/feedback or referring to you for further information) across all Social Media applications; providing analytics data and summary reports to you at a mutually agreed frequency (eg weekly/monthly) and an overview of upcoming planned content/suggested campaigns as required.

I am available to start immediately and as your business grows, I am available to provide additional hours of service if needed.

Please find the attached resume and portfolio for your reference.
I am available to discuss this assignment and gladly answer any questions you may have.

I appreciate you reviewing my proposal, and I look forward to working with you by becoming an exceptional asset to your company.

Thanks,
[name]

[Skype ID]

This person could have been qualified but failed to address the questions in the job post. Instead, he went on and on about his life and personal experience which led me to believe he applies in bulk and won't fit the team well.

A Good Proposal

"financial advisor"

Hello,

Nice to hear about your requirements!

1. I am a SMM expert & the principal of [name of company and website URL included], a Social Media Marketing company. For the past 5 years, I have created and managed 40 Facebook, Twitter, YouTube and Tumblr marketing campaigns for my clients around the world. I can help you build a strong following in the web by creating engaging content, highly effective Facebook/Linkedin/YouTube ad campaign management, creative social media

strategies, increasing page likes/followers/website traffic continuously, digital branding, experience oriented marketing and creating strong brand recall, meaningful engagements with your customers.

2. I am an MBA specializing in Marketing & Finance. I have worked in the financial industry as an adviser (Banking & Insurance) for 4 years. I am qualified Insurance adviser certified by the IRDA (Insurance Regulatory and Development Authority) India

3. 1. Create a positive experience for our audience through FB posts, content,images, ads, etc.,and associate this positive experience with our company brand, thus ensuring high rate of engagements.

   2. Run intuitive Facebook ad campaigns,opinion polls, contests, etc

   3. All the FB posts should include an attractive photo.Visuals creates high rate of audience engagements.

4. [he gave me here three FB pages URLs – as requested]

5. 1.Share interesting latest content related to your domain

   2.Always retweet interesting tweets from our followers and thank them when they retweet our tweets.

   3. Start conversation threads using @ & #

functions thus getting high level of engagements from targeted members & followers of trending topics.

6. I am primarily using Linkedin for b2b campaigns for targeting c-level executives/ decision makers and also evangelizing the brand by participating in communities, discussions, getting connected with new connections etc.

7. Youtube video creation strategies, YouTube advertising using multiple formats, YouTube channel creation and management

I have passed the social media marketing test and U.S. English basic skills test. My skype ID s [Skype ID provided]

Thanks & Regards,
[name]

This freelancer not only read the job post in full—he made the effort to reply to the questions asked by numbering his paragraphs accordingly. This showed me he is very methodical and well organized in his work. He made it to the interview stage. We exchanged a few messages and although he was not the person I hired, his proposal did ensure he would be interviewed for the position.

Another Good Proposal

1. I have about 4+ years of experience in SMM for Enterprise level as well as small & med scale businesses. Understand the fundamentals of Inbound Marketing.

2. Tell us in details what is your financial background and/or experience in relation to financial advisors needs and specifics?

My most recent job was with a leading Mutual fund company based in UK.
They primarily talk about topics like - Financial management tips, Profitable / riskier Investment sectors, Any Financial planning tools that the advisors / direct clients may use for retirement planning / budget, Savings tips, best yields, comment on recent index fluctuations, New rates for their Advisors / wholesale business, talk about no.1 performing product. etc.

Financial Institutions are very careful about there Online Reputation when it and therefore reluctant to adopt riskier marketing techniques as its related to peoples money that they are managing.

3. Give us an example of 3 tactics you employ to increase engagement of the audience on a company FB page
a) Post engaging updates - for e.g. - Ask

opinions, posting Games or Breaking news
b) Use Facebook promotions
c) Timely responses to customer's comments

4. Give us as example 3 FB pages you are particularly proud of - ONLY 3!!!
Sorry, can't share due to NDA with my clients.

5. Give us an example of 3 tactics you employ to increase the friends and followers engagement on a company twitter profile
a) Search for people / groups talking about our company or services.
b) Post relevant twitter updates, share information and #groups.
c) Reply to followers often.

6. What is your experience with LinkedIn? What primarily you have been using it for so far?
Primarily for Networking and Group Discussions.

7. What is your experience on YouTube and how do you decide the course of action there?
I have created and search engine optimized Youtube videos & channels for my clients in the past and then embedded them to various Marketing platforms for Video marketing.

This is the proposal of the freelancer to whom I awarded the job. There were some weak points like abbreviations, incomplete sentences, a few spelling mistakes, and improper usage of subjects or overall sentence structure. However, English is not her mother tongue and the cover letter was more than enough to show me her competences in the financial industry as well as her understanding of social media marketing.

You may notice, as with the previous sample proposal, this applicant also numbered the paragraphs in her application. I am not sure if there is a norm for cover letter writing on Upwork and how numbering paragraphs fits in it, but the numbered paragraphs as well as including my questions along with her answers made it super-easy for me to review her application.

The way she addressed my questions revealed plenty about her personality and ability to follow instructions, loyalty, and work ethics.

I had numbered the questions in the job post, so she mirrored my approach and numbered her answers. This comes to show me she is good at following my lead, which is good because I would be her team leader, if hired.

She not only answered diligently my questions, but she included them along with her answers. This comes to show she pays attention to detail but also, she probably knew I would be reviewing many applications and wanted to make it easy for me to read hers from start to finish without navigating away. My immediate thought was that she appreciated my time and wanted her letter to show a willingness to go a step further to save me some—always a good sign.

She didn't share any FB page examples, as I had asked in the job post, and she apologized, explaining signed nondisclosure agreements (NDA) prevent her from sharing those examples. I respected that and it showed me her work ethics and loyalty to clients.

These were all good traits I was looking for in a team member.

After we exchanged a few messages with follow-up questions and answers, I was convinced she would fit perfectly the team. We worked together on this project for a couple of years and I would be happy to award other projects to her, too.

The given dos and don'ts of proposal writing on Upwork, combined with the sample cover letters I shared with you, should give you enough food for thought how to build your cover letters.

Homework to Practice Proposal Writing

- Open a recent proposal and look for weak areas. Did you follow the instructions of the client in their job post? Did you ask questions? Did you include too much or redundant information? Did you double-check spelling and punctuation before sending? Identify the weak areas and revise the proposal as an exercise. Do this for five proposals you previously sent to clients.

- Look through these five proposals. Is there any information you repeat in each of them? Do you always start your cover letter the same way—

e.g. "Hi, [name], I am suitable for your project because …"? Do you include the same info about your experience—e.g. "I have extensive experience in marketing, including but not limited to strategy planning, social media daily management, e-mail marketing planning …"? Do you end your cover letters the same way—e.g. "Thanks for reading my application. Looking forward to hearing back from you."? If you do, then create a master file with that information and use it each time you apply to a project. Start off from this file and customize it specifically for each project.

- Now open a job post you like and build your proposal by using these guidelines.

- Now do it again with another job post. Then again with yet another job post.

- Seek feedback, where possible, so that you can further improve the way you write your proposals.

STEP 7: OUTPERFORM YOUR INTERVIEW COMPETITION

Conducting a freelance interview is almost always in the best interest of both clients and freelancers. It gives you the chance to land the job, but also to decide whether you truly want to work with that particular client, or not.

The Freelance Interview—Technically Speaking

On Upwork, it is not necessary to have a face-to-face interview. Technically, it's just called an interview so that you can differentiate the projects you have applied to (a.k.a. submitted proposals) from the projects you have been approved for the interviewing process (a.k.a. active candidacies).

Usually the client chooses the best form of conducting the freelance interview. However, if you have preferences, be sure to communicate them. There's no obvious reason for the client to disagree.

The freelance interview gives both parties the opportunity to ask questions and to get the answers they are looking for. During the freelance interview, it's accustomed to negotiate all conditions and requirements of the project—e.g. timeline, deadlines, working hours (if any), online availability (if needed), communication channels, reports, work flow, and so on.

The freelance interview could be conducted via e-mail or in real-time, or both.

In case you choose an e-mail freelance interview, a few e-mails or messages on the website with questions and answers are exchanged, perhaps some documents related to the company and the project, and that's about it.

However, usually the freelance interview is conducted via Skype, Google Hangout, Yahoo Messenger, Upwork messenger or some other platform for real-time communication. It can be chat, voice call, or video conference. The purpose of this form of interview is to ask and answer questions in real- time, to define requirements and expectations, work-flow, etc.

There's added value to this type of freelance interview:

- The client could determine how fluent the freelancer is in English (if it is not their mother tongue).

- Both the client and the freelancer could hear the other party's voice and get a feel of personal qualities like honesty, responsibility, confidence, and others, which you find useful and necessary for a successful collaboration.

If your freelance interview is a voice call, it's recommended you have a headset to improve the call quality. The good sound experience during the call impacts the after-interview feelings of the prospective client.

I prefer voice call interviews both as a client and as a freelancer, so that I can make an informed decision if I want to work with the other party or not. A lot of people can write good proposals or have them written for them, for a fee. In a real-time voice communication though, neither you nor the client can pretend much. For the trained ear, a voice call interview will show the personal qualities of the potential client or freelancer and will help both parties decide if they want to enter a mutual contract.

As for the camera being on or off, it is a matter of personal preference. There are no set rules or etiquette. I don't find video calls necessary as it is not important how the person looks but how they articulate their thoughts and how they behave. You will work with this person online—why do you need to see them?

Many would argue that a lot can be learned from body language. I agree. But you can basically hear if someone is smiling or gesticulating so a video call would add little to the voice call regarding body language.

The same people would argue that a video conference would reveal if the freelancer is dressed professionally and appears to have a decent working space as a home office. True—but is that really important when in a client-freelancer online relationship? For instance, I never dress up for work and my work clothes are often not exactly appropriate for the office. Also, my home office is often outside so what one can see behind me is the sea, a white wall, or just a bunch of trees in the park. Does either of these testify to my skills as a marketer? I don't think so.

I can dress however I want or work wherever I want—that's the beauty of freelancing. And neither my work clothes, nor my "home office" have anything to do with how I do my job and treat clients. So I am sure to keep my camera off at all times. I have never had a video interview with a prospect, and it has never been a reason for not getting a job.

If someone insists on a video call after all and you accept their reasons for the request, you could of course turn your camera on this one time, or for a little while. If there's no good reason for this requirement, and the prospective client refuses a voice call and insists on having a video call instead, watch out—it may be a red flag for a bad client who is too controlling and doesn't respect you as a professional.

You may not be dressed properly. You may be in the middle of a house renovation. You may have unstable internet and a video call would exhaust most of your broadband leaving the internet connection slow and unresponsive for everyone in your household or office. You may just be shy and prefer not to show your face. Whatever the reasons, you have the right to your privacy. Communicate your concern with the prospective client and see how they react.

It's true that working online takes a lot of the personal touch out of the way people interact, but if a client doesn't respect your privacy and wants to have a video call at any cost, you should think well how much this client would respect your time or work ethics and principles, should you start working together.

I am not saying you shouldn't have video calls. If you enjoy seeing the other person while talking to them, please do. What I am saying is be careful and considerate with whom you have video calls and for what reason.

Another important detail of the freelance interview is the non-disclose agreement (NDA). Some clients require their freelancers to sign such a document. Usually, this happens if you will potentially work on a large-scale project with sizable teams. Read it before signing, but don't be put off if a client asks of you to sign an NDA. They are just trying to protect their intellectual property and business information. Note that the NDA should be signed after a job has been awarded to you and before you start working on it.

Asking Questions during the Interview

During your freelance interview, always ask *all* the questions you have regarding the project and the company. Never enter a contract with any outstanding questions.

When I am looking for freelancers on Upwork (marketers, writers, virtual assistants, designers, programmers), only rarely will someone ask me a question. I write detailed enough job posts but still—there is plenty of room for questions if the applicant is truly interested. Almost no one asks questions, let alone relevant and smart ones.

Know that asking questions doesn't make you look stupid or incompetent, to the contrary. Similarly to writing proposals, asking questions during the interview shows engagement and demonstrates you have put some thought into the project. You already see yourself working on it. That will help you stand apart from the crowd.

Industry specifics and important project details vary for different types of professionals—e.g. one thing is important for designers, another for programmers, third thing for writers, fourth thing for marketers, and so on. However, there are questions which must be asked and answered during the interviewing process and before taking up a new client, regardless the profession and industry.

Project Duration

Every client who knows what they want and need should be able to say if the project is a quick job (less than a month duration), short term (one to six months), or long term (more than six months).

Depending on your current workload and plans for the coming months, you can decline a project based solely on its expected duration.

For example, I remember a few years ago one of my favorite projects was stopped due to insufficient funding. I was waiting for the project to be restarted. I didn't have clarity about when that might happen, but I knew something was cooking. So I wanted to make sure I would be available when it was back on the table and hiring.

For that reason, there was a time when I took new projects only if they required a month or less to complete. Isn't it wonderful how flexible freelancing is?

Estimated Workload

Combined with the first question about the project duration, this may be a deal breaker sometimes.

Ask the client if you are expected to work ten or forty hours per week.

Ask also if there are any requirements about time slots you should be available online—e.g. every work day from 2:00 to 4:00 p.m. Eastern Time in Skype. This adds up to ten hours per week, which may be a suitable workload for your schedule. However, you lose your flexibility. It's a set time slot every day Monday through Friday. This is a deal breaker for me, but it might be convenient for you. It's a matter of preference.

My point is, whatever the case, such requirements should be communicated before you enter a contract. If the client didn't say anything about it, ask them, just to make sure.

Project Goals and Your Role

If your prospective client cannot answer what their project goals are or what your role in the project is, you have a potential problem on your hands. Let me give you an example.

Let's say you will have to write two blog posts per week for the next six months.

You should know in advance what the purpose of this content is—to inform, to motivate the reader for some type of action, to entertain, to help with branding, improve SEO rankings, all of these, something else.

You should also know if you will be given an audience profile or you will have to research that on your own (or even worse, you will have to write blindly without any information about your readers whatsoever.)

Another thing you'd want to know is if you will be provided with topics and writing briefs or if you will be doing that, too. Is there a blog editorial calendar? How many edits are included in the price of a blog post? What is the editing process (if any)? Do you just write or also upload your blog posts to the blog platform the client uses? What about contextual images and formatting?

All of these details should be discussed and agreed on *before* you enter a contract. If the client has difficulties answering any of these questions or is unwilling to think about them before you start a contract, beware—you risk having a lot of work which doesn't have anything to do with writing and quite possibly isn't paid for either.

Payment

The question about payment is also bound to be asked and answered during the freelance interview. Assuming you have the answers to the above questions, it shouldn't be hard to answer this one either.

If hired by the hour, you should be able to estimate how much time it will take to do a certain task. Note it is an estimation—after all, hiring by the hour gives the client the flexibility to ask you to redo work as much as they please, to assign additional tasks (if you have the availability), and so on.

If hired on a fixed-price job, like per blog post or per month, you should be very clear what's included in the price and what the payment schedule is. Negotiate milestone payments. Those are covered by escrow service on Upwork. Just make sure the client funds each milestone before you start working on it, and that you submit your work through Upwork to automatically request funds release.

Work Delivery

Another question to ask during the freelance interview is about presenting your work.

If you are charging by the hour and your work is ongoing, negotiate a reporting system and schedule. Depending on workload and work complexity, you can report daily, weekly, or monthly via e-mail, phone, or Skype. It all depends on you and your clients' preferences.

If the project is short-term and/or fixed price—e.g. for five blog posts, one website design, iPhone application development, or anything else which is measured by quantity and not work hours, there are plenty of details you should discuss and agree on, such as:

- **Time frame for a first draft**—you can even make a milestone payment out of it.

- **Time frame for feedback on that first draft and edit requests, if any**—I can only imagine you don't want to submit your first draft and then hang in uncertainty for three weeks because the client has forgotten they hired you at all, let alone the need of feedback about your first draft.

- **Deadline for final draft submission**—remember you should have also negotiated the number of edits included in your price quote.

Always submit your completed work through the Upwork milestones system so that work approval and funds release is automatically requested upon work delivery. Even if your client does not manually release the payment for whatever reason, the system will automatically do so in fourteen days, but only if you have requested the payment through the Upwork milestone system.

The Client's Website URL

If you have not received it before the freelance interview, you definitely should get it during the interview.

If they don't have a website yet and the project you apply to is for its creation, then ask for social media profiles of their executive team, partners' feedback and testimonials, anything. It is highly unlikely there's someone without a digital profile today so do your homework. Before saying yes to this new client, find out with whom you are dealing.

Specific Questions about the Work Itself

All specific questions about the work itself should also be asked during the freelance interview.

If something is not clear as early as now, make sure to ask your prospect to clarify or further explain. **Never enter a contract on a project you still have questions about.**

Depending on your line of work and the specific project being interviewed for, these will be different. Let me give you an example of a project I discussed with a client recently.

The client approached me because he needed help with his LinkedIn page. He didn't give me any information about his company or the goals he had in mind for his LinkedIn page, but he gave me the URL of the page. From there I found his website and other social media profiles related to his company.

I explained what I could do for him in the context of my availability and expertise, and also what I would need from him as information to give him a price quote and to map the steps toward project completion. The questions I asked were:

- What is your target audience?

- Who are your top three competitors?

- What's your unique selling proposition and your value proposition?

- What are your company's existing marketing communication programs?

- What are the goals you want to achieve with this project?

- What is your budget for the project?

To each question, I attached a detailed explanation why I asked the question as well as instructions on how he could best answer each one.

For example, when I asked him about the target audience, I included a template for an audience profile and the steps he needed to take in order to give me a snapshot of his audience. I also directed him on how to do this for all segments of his market.

I could tell he was already sold on me by the way I handled this preliminary communication. It was evident he wasn't used to someone asking questions and planning their work so well ahead of time before even landing the project.

Answering Questions during the Interview

Asking prospective clients some questions is as important as addressing their questions during the interview. In my experience, clients ask three types of questions, depending how experienced they are in conducting interviews.

General Questions

The majority of clients on Upwork ask general questions. They may or may not have experience in conducting interviews with freelancers. They are more likely not experts in your field, regardless your profession. The purpose of their questions is to see how you conduct yourself when communicating with others.

Are you fluent in English? Do your thoughts flow smoothly? Are you persuasive? Do you have charisma? Will you work well together due to matching communication skills?

General questions I have been asked usually gravitate around the work I do and why I think I am suitable for their project.

For example, when I apply to a SMM strategy planning project, clients often ask me to explain the difference between social media networks, why I think one is better than the other for their project, what would a SMM strategy plan include, what level of detail I would provide in the plan, would I be able to carry it out or do I need to form a team afterwards to train and/or manage, and so on.

In these situations when the client asks general questions you can really shine by asking your own questions, specifically for the project, because the client will see not only you are the professional you claim to be, but your ability to think on your feet and to apply your professional knowledge in real-life situation such as their project.

Project-Specific Questions

Clients with extensive experience in working with virtual teams usually ask project-specific questions. They may ask general questions as well but what differentiates them from most clients on Upwork is that they know what they are looking for and ask questions which only suitable applicants will be able to address. Clients who ask such questions are usually good clients looking for quality work and a long-term relationship.

To continue the above example with a client in need of SMM strategist, I can tell you that the client most probably would ask all the general questions outlined above but also, something about the best approach *in their industry* for LI marketing—is LI a suitable channel and why? How would you go about growing *their* company page following? Why would you recommend a certain direction? Should they optimize their personal LI profiles, how and why? Will LI group discussions be part of the marketing mix and why? What LI groups would you recommend they use and why? What topics would you discuss on LI?

Some clients may give hypothetical situations and ask how you'd go about the plan, should you be hired. For example, they might tell you they are a small business opening a new store in city X. Their target audience consists of mothers between thirty-five and forty-five who have an interest in gardening, most probably running a blog of some kind and owning a business. Then the client lets you know the goal is to grow their LI page following to increase the bottom line of their business, so they then ask what you would do to achieve that goal.

On one hand, you could suggest the best policy is to optimize their personal profile and use LI groups and proactive networking on a profile-to-profile basis to build meaningful relationships and grow their personal network. You will guide them how to use the search feature on LI to find suitable connections, following their target audience profile specifics. But you can also ask follow-up questions like do they have budget for LI advertising? Do they have a blog and should you build relationships with bloggers? Maybe some of them could be brand ambassadors which in turn would help you reach a larger audience? Does the client plan to sell only offline in their new store or are they also interested in promoting their online store? What is the goal specifically (Y% increase in revenue by this and this date) and do they know how to track the performance of LI as a communication channel?

The beauty of such project-specific interviews is that usually the client who conducts them is an expert in the field. He or she has already figured out the answers and asks only to see the way you think. Most often there is no right or wrong answer but rather a reality check if your work ethics and style are a good match with the client's preference. The applicants who are invited to such interviews are a very short list, and you either compete with one or two other freelancers or don't compete with anyone at all.

Be careful not to spend too much time on preparation before getting hired though. Don't spend hours to research the industry and to come up with a detailed plan about their LI company page and personal profile. You can address the project specific questions by doing the analysis of the situation while you speak. If unsure of something, say so and explain why answering such questions would require some research time, which you'd gladly spend if hired. After all, the idea of these interviews is not to give the client their strategy but to show you are an expert in your field and you know what is required to get the job done.

Performance-Based Questions

It is very rare to encounter a client on Upwork who asks performance-based questions. It has happened to me only a couple of times in my freelance practice.

I was once asked to give a real-life example where I helped another client start their activities on LI; what tactics I used to build a strong network of connections and to attract followers to their page and most importantly, what effect that had on the business bottom line.

I was not able to share all the details of that real-life example due to signed NDA, but nevertheless I could and I did share some details without revealing any information which is protected under the NDA.

I described the company and its market position, as well as the starting point of the project, the goal, and what tactics I used to achieve the goal.

Performance-based questions aim not so much at getting the details of a past job, but rather how you work and how well you'll fit the team if hired. Answers to such questions reveal work ethics, whether you possess the needed skills to carry out the project, and what value you will add to the company. Clients want to make sure that you are not speaking only in theory but have the hard data to back up your claims.

These examples are marketing specific but that's because I am a marketing consultant. The same principles apply for any profession. By following the logic I laid out, you should be able to figure out what the general, project-specific or performance-based questions would be in your profession and niche of expertise for any given project.

Good Practices for Your Freelance Interview

Now that you know how important asking questions is, and what type of questions to expect—let's shed some light on other best practices to further help you outperform the competition during the interview.

Write Down Your Questions

Before going to the freelance interview, look again at the job post. See what preliminary information the client has given. If there's something unclear or contradictory, draft your questions on a sheet of paper or a new Word document.

Writing down your questions in advance will help you stay on topic. Even if the client steers the conversation in a different direction, you can always look at the notes and get back on track with your questions.

Get an Idea Who Will Be Interviewing You

Some companies who hire freelancers on Upwork have a project manager do their recruiting. Others have dedicated HR departments. And yet others are just a one-man show and do everything themselves—that's why they are looking for help.

If possible, find out who'll be interviewing you and find as much info about them as possible. Are they a creative person, a manager, an HR specialist, experienced in conducting freelance interviews or a newbie? Someone else?

Here's an example how this information could help. If interviewed by a seasoned HR specialist, you should answer questions humbly and ask yours when given the opportunity. You should also be prepared for project-specific questions or even a performance-based interview. If you are interviewed by someone who has not conducted many interviews, maybe they'll ask only general questions. It could be better if you take a leading role during the interview. This way you'll demonstrate how well versed you are as a freelancer who works in an online environment.

Always Reply in a Timely Manner

If the prospective client accepts your application and sends a message, try to reply within twenty-four hours.

The same time frame is recommended if invited to bid on a freelance project—try to accept or decline that invitation within twenty-four hours. This way you show availability and interest toward the project.

If you don't want to address work-related e-mails during weekends (I don't), then try to reply within one business day. Make sure you tell the prospective client why your reply is delayed, especially if you have a big time difference. It will show them you have set working hours and should they need something, they shouldn't expect it on your days off.

Nevertheless, know that clients frown upon taking a few days to reply to a single message. It means you are not interested or you just lack time management skills. If you delay your reply for some reason, always apologize for the delay and if appropriate and relevant, explain your reasons.

Be Honest and Genuine

Nobody likes a fake person who will do whatever it takes to make themselves look good. I have encountered my fair share of freelancers who say yes to everything I ask, only to find out after I hire them that they cannot deliver anything as per our preliminary agreement—be it time frame or quality.

With time, I learned to spot those freelancers instantly. So chances are your prospects will too if you try to oversell yourself.

Don't say you have a skill if you don't. Don't accept a job you are not sure how you will complete. And certainly don't rely on a friend's help. Don't pretend to be someone you are not. In the end, it will only waste your client's time and money and will hurt your reputation.

Homework to Improve Interview Performance

For the purposes of this exercise, take one of your active candidacies. If you don't have any, pick a project already applied to and pretend your proposal has been accepted.

- Draft the questions you want to ask the client during the interview.

- Research who will be interviewing you and decide on the best approach (follow their lead or take a leading role during the interview if they lack experience); start from their job post and work your way up, based on the information you already have about the prospect (website URL, name, etc.)

- Decide which personal qualities your prospect will appreciate the most. Write them down and include notes how those qualities add value to your potential client's team. Remember, be genuine. Don't pretend you are someone you are not.

- Draft some expected general questions and think about the answers you'd give.

- Draft some project-specific questions and brainstorm ideas how to reply.

- Draft some performance-based questions as well, should you be interviewed by an HR specialist. Think back—what similar projects have you completed before? Look through your documents and draft some details to share, if asked.

- Do this for five more projects. If needed, find a friend or a colleague who has more experience with interviews—practice with them. Practice makes perfect.

NINE HARD TRUTHS YOU NEED TO KNOW NOW

There are some hard truths you need to know to sustain a successful freelance practice. All of these I found out the hard way when I was starting. Knowing them as early as now will prepare you for the (sometimes bumpy) road that lies ahead.

Being a successful freelancer is not only about landing the project and doing your job well. It has its ups and downs. You, and *only you*, are responsible for both your success and your failure, which can be a double-edged sword. This section of the book aims at helping you be a better freelancer in order to more fully enjoy the freelance lifestyle, at all times.

Hard Truth #1

Sometimes you will feel miserable and it is paramount that even then you stay determined and never give up.

I am 100% sure that at some point, you will feel desperate. You will be angry with some low-paid contractors who work for $3 per hour and (you think) because of them, you can't land any projects. You'll be tired of reading job posts and writing custom proposals for every project of interest. You'll be wondering if it was a mistake to go freelance. You'll feel small and incompetent. You'll have tons of doubts.

I *know* this—I was in that situation when I was starting.

As bad as it all seems at that moment, STAY ON COURSE! (Sorry for shouting but it IS important you hear me!)

The sun always comes up, right? Your time will come, too.

There are enough clients and work for all freelancers. Someday a client will give you a first chance. Then you'll get a second one, a third one, and before you even know it, you will have so many invitations and offers in your mailbox that you won't have enough time to read them all and decline.

The only thing required is to *stay on course*. Do not give up before you even started. Don't take rejection personally. Don't let your weak moments dictate your freelance future.

Here's a secret—when I was feeling down in the beginning and questioning everything, I always asked **why I am doing this**.

What do I want? Will I get it if I don't do this? What do I need to do to get it? Usually, when I answered honestly all three questions, I had completed my reality check and was ready to read through some more project descriptions and send another proposal.

Learning to overcome the urge to give up will help you later to be a successful freelancer.

Hard Truth #2

Being a freelancer is hard.

From the outside, being a (successful) freelancer may seem super-easy:

- You get up from bed whenever you feel like it (to the envy of friends).

- You work on what you like and whenever you please.

- You choose with whom you work.

- You travel a lot (if you want to).

- You always seem smiling and stress-free ...

Well, the latter pretty much depends on your line of work but generally speaking, being a freelancer also means a way lower stress level than the average office employee. All of this, and I really mean *all* of this, is absolutely true, but it also has its price.

Being a freelancer = self-discipline + good planning + superb time management

Let me repeat that—self-discipline, good planning, and superb time management are crucial for the success of any freelancer. In the next sections you'll learn more about these but let me say this: you (a.k.a. the freelancer) are both the boss and the employee.

You give the orders and you follow them. There is no one else to blame for a delay if one occurs. You are the one making the decisions and taking responsibility for your own actions. You wear all the hats, and you are the one your client looks at with gratitude for the successful project ... or with disappointment for the huge failure their project turned out to be.

Being a freelancer also equals determination, persistence, and patience

You need determination so that you send out twenty proposals in one day, all of them perfect.

You need persistence to send out twenty more perfect proposals the next day, although you never received a reply on any of your first twenty cover letters.

And finally, you need patience because the project manager whose project you have liked so much always has something more important to do than reading proposals and getting in touch with you for the job.

I don't have any tips for you how to develop determination, persistence, and patience. I have always been determined. Persistence and patience I learned through practice and continuously reminding myself why I am trying to become a freelancer.

Hard Truth #3

You need specific qualities to succeed as a freelancer.

As we established already, being a freelancer is not easy. Here are the top-ten qualities and personal traits needed to succeed as a freelancer. *Note that most, if not all, of these qualities can be acquired. If you don't have them now, you certainly should make the effort to develop them (if you want to succeed, that is).*

Self-discipline

Maybe this is the most important quality as without it, you would never be able to handle work and life as a freelancer.

Self-discipline is when you get up at nine in the morning although you don't have anywhere to be, but do it anyway because there are so many clients who don't know you exist yet and might be needing just the service you have to offer.

Self-discipline is when nobody returns your e-mails and despite that, you still find the strength to open Upwork and send more proposals to more new clients only because you said to yourself you have to.

Self-discipline is when a friend invites you to the movies and you decline because you have not sent enough proposals that day, or you have a deadline to keep the next day.

As a freelancer you will have plenty of opportunities to do interesting and fun things, things you like. You'll be tempted to do them every time an opportunity presents itself. And if you do, you'll end up playing chess, walking the dog, drinking beer, and whatever else you like doing literally all day.

But then, while you're having fun, work will suffer. You'll miss deadlines, upset clients, and lose clients and money. Having fun all the time is always at the cost of a job well done.

Setting a schedule for the day and the week is paramount for the organization of daily activities—work or play. Keeping that schedule requires self-discipline.

Persistence

Being a freelancer can be extremely hard sometimes, especially in the beginning when your e-mail inbox is full of rejection letters and not interview invitations. Not to mention your goal to actually land a job.

Persistence is when you receive a rejection letter and send two more proposals right that hour.

Persistence is when you go to the next interview although you failed miserably on the last one.

Persistence is when you re-do your work for the third time, only to prove to your very first client you are worthy of the chance they gave you.

It is of crucial importance to believe in yourself, your skills, and your abilities.

It is of crucial importance to not give up when the road is steep or bumpy.

It is of crucial importance to be persistent and to not stop looking for clients. You will need just one or two to notice you and give you a chance to prove yourself. Then it gets easier.

Time Management Skills

This is not about working hours. It is about estimation—how much time what type of task would take; how many tasks you can complete per day or for a certain period of time, and so on.

Good time management is estimating two hours and fifteen minutes for that one task, and when done, you look at the clock and it has been exactly two hours and fifteen minutes since you started.

Good time management is when you are never late for an interview or a meeting with a client.

Good time management is when you don't miss deadlines.

Planning time wisely and following that plan are of crucial importance for productivity. If done well, your clients will be happy and so will you in the end of the workday or week.

(In the next hard truth section in the book you will find some tips how to instantly improve your time management skills.)

Professionalism

If you want to be treated like a freelance consultant and not like an employee, you need to prove independency and earn the trust of your clients. Being professional is the best policy. What does this mean?

Professionalism is when you address your prospective client's questions before they have even thought of asking them.

Professionalism is when you keep your nerve when a client is unreasonable or unprofessional.

Professionalism is when you give your best to that old client although he pays twice less than your newest one.

To sum it up in a few words, professional freelancers let their work speak for them:

- They always do their job on time and with the agreed quality.

- They keep their promises and honor the preliminary agreements with their clients.

- They communicate well and in a timely manner.

- They are honest.

- They are ethical.

Basically, this is everything that you, as a freelancer, would expect from your clients.

Initiative

If you have been an employee for a long time in the "wrong company," you may be used to being dependent. For example, you may find it normal to have someone constantly checking up on you, following every step, verifying your work, and telling you what to do.

The moment you become a freelancer, you have clients and not "keepers" who call themselves "the boss." You no longer will be told what to do. You need to take initiative.

Initiative is when a proposal includes an idea how the project can be improved without the prospective client asking you to do it, such as while writing their website content you also make sure it's optimized for search engines.

Initiative is when you suggest hiring a virtual assistant to help the CEO because you see they are always behind schedule due to a huge e-mail backlog. You even recommend someone.

Initiative is when your client's website is down and, although you are not his webmaster and your job has nothing to do with website maintenance, you pick up the phone and tell him about the problem.

You need to ask questions. You need to suggest ways to improve the project and the overall outcome. Clients value such behavior.

When you show initiative, you demonstrate interest in completing the project on time and with high quality. And who knows, maybe this client will give you another project soon enough.

Having Principles

Nobody likes to be misled or lied to, especially if they pay for high quality work and professional consultation. Being a freelancer, it is your responsibility to do your job. If you compromise on your principles once, I promise it won't be the last time.

You will start working with clients who are twisting your arm for money, control, low-quality work for less money, and more. There are plenty of possible scenarios.

Having principles is when you decline a project because the client refuses to pay fair rates.

Having principles is when you refuse to negotiate or meet with clients who ignore your questions and expect you to be available 24/7 because you don't have any work at the moment.

Having principles is when even though you don't have any current clients, you refuse to market a product which is purposefully misleading to its intended audience.

The only way to keep your reputation intact and to reduce (if not eliminate) the stress at your work place is to stand by your principles, always.

When I was starting, nobody told me how important work principles were to freelance success. I will show you how to figure out yours in one of the next hard truth sections.

Determination

Unless you commit to succeed, you won't make it as a freelancer. No matter who tells you what, you should believe in your skills and in your bright future as a freelancer.

Determination is when your family tells you to get a "real job" on a daily basis and despite that, you keep on sending proposals and communicating with clients to prove that working from home is as real a job as it gets.

Determination is when you don't succumb to the pressure of not having any interviews for a week and keep on going forward, thinking of the freedom you'll eventually have once you succeed as a freelancer.

Determination is when you finally land your first client and do the impossible to keep them as a long-term one through outstanding service and being trusted.

If you don't think you have it in you, don't worry. Determination comes with practice. When you figure out your principles, standing your ground when communicating with clients will teach you determination, too.

Responsibility

As a freelancer, you will often have to make decisions and take responsibility for your actions. You will have to own both your successes and your failures. You will benefit from the ability to assess the situation and make decisions on the spot, too.

Responsibility is when you decline a project offer because you lack a certain skill that would prevent you from doing an awesome job.

Responsibility is when you are 100% honest in your proposals and don't try to game the system by cheating on your skill test or lying to your clients about your competencies.

Responsibility is when you make a mistake and admit it to yourself or your client. Then find what went wrong, draw your conclusions, and make sure it never happens again.

If you have not yet developed a good sense of responsibility, don't worry. Your work will teach you. This ability comes with experience. When you do have it, it will definitely be to your advantage. Good clients seek and appreciate responsibility.

Flexibility

Being flexible will help in situation assessment and decision-making. It will also help when diversifying your portfolio and skills, and when looking for new opportunities and freelance trends.

Flexibility is when a client calls last minute with a rush job and you cancel your girls' or boys' night out to accommodate his urgent need because he has no one else to turn to for help.

Flexibility is when you've been doing social media marketing for a while and a new social network emerges causing your client to ask you to look into it and see how their business can benefit from being among the first on it. It's not your specialty—nevertheless, you decide to change directions to help a client in need.

Flexibility is when your laptop breaks down in the worst possible moment when you have a tight deadline. You go to your sister's house in the middle of the night to use her computer only to keep your deadline.

Flexibility will help you analyze information and adapt; learn new things if the workforce market demands it.

Also, your flexibility will allow you to take rush jobs from clients. Last-minute tasks are not mandatory, of course—you can always decline if not available; or to ask for more money.

However, if you are flexible and do the job despite the short notice and the quick turnaround time, this client will appreciate it and will remember it. They will call again because they will know they can rely on you in hard times, too.

Effective Communication Skills

Effective communication takes place only when the listener clearly understands the message that the speaker intended to send.

In most cases, freelancers on Upwork work exclusively online. So the main communication channel is e-mail, chat, voice or video calls, and similar programs, always through a computer. Therefore, the communication should be well thought and precise, at all times.

Effective communication is when you don't assume anything—you always ask when something isn't clear.

Effective communication is when you don't take feedback or rejection personally. The other party critiques your work, not you as a person. Don't get angry with them—don't insult them. Learn from it.

Effective communication is when a client asks a question but you need extra time to research the answer, and you e-mail them back quickly, saying they will receive their answer in three days.

Many clients are not effective communicators. Deal with it by being an effective communicator yourself. Address questions in a timely manner. And if the client wants changes, always have a written confirmation.

Hard Truth #4

You need excellent time management skills to succeed as a freelancer.

The requirement for time management skills isn't just a trend seen in clients' job posts. As a freelancer, you need to organize your work process and to complete projects with quality in the agreed time frame. To get you started, here are ten tips to instantly improve your time management and productivity.

Learn to Prioritize

It's super-important to decide what to put on the top of your to-do list. Decide which tasks are more important than others and what should be done when.

No, they are not all urgent. And no, they should not all be done today. Think about your pending tasks and arrange them on your to-do list according to their priority.

For many people it is easier to complete tasks if they have a numbered list of to-dos on their desk. It is especially true when these tasks are work-related.

Write down your to-do list—first, second, third, and so on. Start from the top. Complete one task at a time. Sooner or later all to-dos will be crossed off. The key is to consistently and continuously work on a single task at a time.

This was true for me, too. But now, I don't care much about simple to-do lists. I cannot live without my Google calendar (see Appendix 2: URL References). I have found that adding to my calendar fun activities like a walk in the park or bike trip to the nearby village helps me stay on track with my work tasks as well.

Find what works for you and tweak it when necessary to make it better.

Plan Your Tasks for the Week

And when I say plan I don't mean think about it and have an idea about what is it that you need to do the next few days. Monday morning (or better yet, Friday afternoon, right before you close the shop for the week), write down all the tasks you have to do next week—per day, even per hour if you can.

You can plan your week using pen and paper, time planner of some kind, Google calendar, Outlook calendar or any type of application, program or platform to your liking. Write them down—this is key.

Only if written down, you will have an exact idea at a glance what you have to do when. This way you will be able to focus on following the plan and implementing the tasks.

Also, track your time to improve your estimations. Often you think a task will take you so much time but in reality, it takes twice as much. With practice, you'll develop a great sense of how long different tasks take, but only if you purposefully pay attention to it.

Always Leave a Time Buffer

Never fill working hours to 100% so that you are flexible at all times.

If you have a time buffer, you will be able to:

- Do a last-minute rush job for a regular client.

- Do a couple more edits of that monthly newsletter because the client remembered a webinar announcement they wanted to include.

- Hand in your work on time although the research needed was a few hours longer than anticipated.

These are hypothetical situations, but you get the idea why building a time buffer is important. Worst case scenario—if nothing unforeseen happens—you will have some more me-time on your hands.

Check Your E-mail Once or Twice per Day

Often people get addicted to their e-mails and hit the refresh button constantly—on the laptop, on the cell phone while waiting in line, while having coffee at the local café, before lunch, during lunch, after lunch ... I know, I've been there.

There is nothing you'd get via e-mail that couldn't wait for a few hours. E-mail is one of those low-priority tasks which has no place on top of your to-do list.

Build a habit to check your e-mail once or twice per day. Find your best time to do that.

I do it in the morning and in the afternoon. Many people say it isn't a good idea to check e-mail in the morning because you get sucked in and can waste a good two hours purging e-mails—and those often are your most productive hours. However, I am in Europe and the majority of my clients are in North America. So I have made it a habit to check my e-mail in the morning but only to see if there is something new from my clients on the other side of the ocean. Maybe while I was sleeping, they were working.

All other e-mails can wait for my afternoon e-mail checkup. There are exceptions of course. Some days I am involved in heavy e-mail back and forth correspondence. In those days I check my e-mail way more often than twice per day and it shows as my productivity falls immensely.

Bottom line, find what works for you and stick to it. Don't check your e-mail all the time. Build habits around your time zone and your clients' time zones. Get your clients used to the idea you reply to e-mails within a business day and not within thirty minutes. This will enable you to focus on your work. And by the way, it will also decrease the number of rush jobs which aren't urgent at all.

Turn Off Your Chat Programs

Skype, Yahoo Messenger, Google Hangout, HipChat, or whatever else instant messaging program you use—they are all a huge distraction.

Here is an innocent conversation:

> - Hey, you, how are you?

> - I am fine, and you?

> - I am great, big news—have to see you! Want to have coffee tomorrow?

> - Sure, 10 am at the coffee shop on 5th?

> - Great, can't wait—see you then!

What seems an innocent quick chat can destroy your concentration.

First, you had to stop doing whatever you were doing and agree on a time and a place for that meeting with this other person. And second, your mind is probably now thinking of scenarios what this great news is that begs for having coffee and talking about it and not sharing it immediately on Skype. So, what are you doing—working or thinking about tomorrow's coffee and news?

You have been waiting and searching for inspiration for hours. At last it came only to leave in the middle of your first sentence, when the next instant message comes in and you are too curious not to look.

So, while doing creative work, it is better to turn off communication channels with the rest of the world. If you think you'd need Skype for a quick work-related question at some point, at least put up a "Do not disturb" message so other people won't distract you.

Spend Less Time on Social Media

Social media is a time-wasting machine. Don't log in to your Facebook profile every five minutes. If it's on your bookmarks tab, remove it right this moment. I used to spend a lot of time on Facebook, but I finally kicked the habit when I removed it from my bookmarks tab. If something important happens, I bet you will hear about it on the phone anyway.

Your daily horoscope won't change the course of the day; neither will your virtual fortune cookie. Not to mention how insignificant to your well-being is John's Facebook farm (yes, remember John, your classmate from second grade?) You anyway don't know what's with his constant neighbor harvest requests.

Break the Bad Habit of Procrastination

Every once in a while we all procrastinate. Yes, I do, too. Sometimes.

I have noticed it is a common habit of nine-to-five employees to leave work for tomorrow. Something like why-I-should-do-this-today-if-I-can-do-it-tomorrow mentality.

Freelancers are not employees. As a freelancer, you don't have a boss who cares mostly about punch-in and punch-out times. You don't have a supervisor who thinks time spent in the office equals completed work. You have clients who want you to complete work with quality and on time.

As a freelancer, you should care about the quality and turnaround time of your work. You put your name and reputation on the line every time you take up a project and deliver the end result. If it's good—it's good. If not—well, as I said, it's your name on the line.

Unless you are sick or totally lack focus or inspiration, do not leave work for tomorrow if you planned to do it today.

Maybe tomorrow you will need that time buffer you left when planning your workload for the week for some unforeseen last-minute edits or design changes. Or maybe a long-forgotten friend will call you out of the blue with the unbelievable opportunity to go to Vegas on his expense. Now wouldn't you hate to miss this only because you were too lazy yesterday to do your job the way you planned it in the first place?

Create Rituals to Set the Right Tone

No special clothing is required. Rituals help you focus.

For example, as I said, I check my e-mail while I have my morning coffee. I look through my daily tasks and rearrange them as needed if something urgent has come up during the night. Once I do this, my brain tunes into working mode and I start completing task after task.

But this is specifically for me because, as I said, most of my clients are overseas and we have a relatively big time difference.

Find the rituals that help you focus. They may or may not be work-related. For example, maybe taking a quick shower before you start working helps you focus; or walking the dog first thing in the morning energizes you. The purpose of the rituals is to set the right tone for your workday.

Make Small Steps Every Day

If you are one of those people who always want to do everything here and now, listen up. It is a mission impossible. Don't even think about it! If you put yourself in such a situation, chances are you will end up stressed out, disappointed with yourself, and terrified with your never-ending to-do list.

Break up tasks into smaller and manageable ones. This way, if you get off a task (it happens, and often), you won't let it throw the whole day off schedule. Keep control over your calendar.

When you make small steps, at the end of the day you will turn off the computer and close your to-do list with a smile. You feel empowered that today you did what you wanted to do. You will even expect the next day with excitement because you know tomorrow you will achieve another small victory over your to-do list, just like you did today.

Be Realistic and Forget the Guilt Trips

Going after those small victories on a daily basis shouldn't mislead you though. Be realistic when setting your daily goals and planning your to-dos for the day.

Set the goals too low and you risk being stuck at the point where you do the bare minimum and feel good with mediocre work. Set the goals too high and you risk chasing your tail all day without making any real progress.

If you try to do a month's worth work in a single day, you won't cross any to-dos off of your list; you won't feel satisfied at the end of the day, and you won't have acquired any new skills. You will be trapped by your own ambition and unrealistic self-assessment.

Avoid any guilt-trips when turning off the computer in the afternoon with ten more pending to-dos. It's okay—you can do them tomorrow, or the day after that, or the day after that, depending on their priority.

There will always be more work to be done than you can complete today. The sooner you realize and accept this, the better you'll feel and the more work you'll do in a single day, every day.

Keep Improving Your Time Management Skills

This is not a tip, per se, but it's a good reminder. Time management should be an ongoing process. The better you do it, the better balance you will enjoy in life, and the happier your clients will be. Always look for ways to improve time management skills.

Hard Truth #5

Set working hours helps you succeed.

A step forward to further improving time management skills, among other things, is setting your working hours. Here's how fixed working hours can help you succeed.

Increased Productivity

Yes, you read it right—fixed freelance working hours increase productivity.

I hear you wonder, "What do you mean fixed working hours? That's what I am trying to avoid when leaving the office and going freelance!" True, but not entirely.

First, as a freelancer you have the freedom to decide which part of the day to work and how much. Second, you can always skip a working day or be late for work for whatever reason. So you have all that you wished for when you left your day job.

Setting fixed freelance working hours is for planning purposes. It aims at increasing productivity and improving time management. This way, you avoid splitting time too much during the day and risking finishing nothing come its end.

Besides, you don't overwork yourself. Fixing working hours helps you better plan work for the day and for the week. This in turn ensures you always meet deadlines without pressure or stress. Your clients are happy and your reputation is intact.

More Free Time

The sooner you finish work for the day, the more free time you'll have afterwards.

I used to like sleeping till noon. Naturally, getting up early in the morning to go to the office was my worst nightmare. However, there are a couple of benefits if you choose to start working as a freelancer early in the morning. For instance, if you make it a habit getting up as early as 8:30 a.m., starting work by 9:30 a.m. and working until 1-2 p.m., you free up your afternoon for various activities—sports, a walk in the park, meeting with friends, or whatever else you like doing.

These are four to five hours of active work, during which you'll get more tasks done and have more free time afterwards than if you wake up at noon, go out from time to time, and work in between.

Now, provided you are just starting a freelance career, you may be working on making a name for yourself way more than four to five hours per day. And you will definitely have to commit *all* your working hours for a few months to looking for work and from time to time, actually working. When you have a few complete projects under your belt and clients start finding you, then you can spend most of those four to five hours a day working and just an hour or so every day in reviewing project invitations and talking to prospective clients.

Better Health

Let's face it, if healthy, you are more likely to sustain a successful freelance practice and lifestyle, wouldn't you agree?

Think about your health—work during the day, sleep at night. Don't turn the day into night and vice versa. The freedom to not go to the office could tempt night owls to work at night, but I think that's not a good idea.

First, you'll work only with bad light and risk worsening your eyesight. It's bad enough you already work on a computer all the time.

Second, you risk isolating yourself from family and friends because they sleep at night and play during the day while you work at night and sleep during the day.

Active Social Life

Maintaining an active social life is especially important when you lack colleagues to share your morning coffee time.

You like Spanish? Enroll in a Spanish class every Tuesday and Friday—you will learn the language, meet like-minded people in class, and finally go to Spain to practice your new language and to learn more about their culture.

You miss your office colleagues? Call them and go to lunch. It doesn't mean you can't hang with them if you no longer work at their office.

You miss the office noise? Find a coffee shop with good Wi-Fi and work from there every Monday. Locate the nearest co-working space in your town and go mingle (and work) there every Wednesday. Get creative—where else you have dreamt of working from? Now is the time to try and do it.

Find a hobby, meet like-minded people, travel. These will make you a better person *and* a better freelancer. But you will be able to squeeze these activities in your work day only if you have set working hours and have developed good time management skills.

Consistency with Your Clients

If you have fixed freelance working hours, you develop working habits and are available to your clients at certain times on a regular basis. This way they know when you work and when not; they have their expectations and know when to turn to you for help. More importantly, they know when to expect your reply. You come across as reliable.

For example, if your working hours are all over the place, you risk being bombarded with "important" and "urgent" requests all the time and if you cannot meet an unrealistic deadline, the clients are not happy.

However, if you work Monday through Friday, 9:00 a.m. to 2:00 p.m., your clients know that if they e-mail you on a Friday late afternoon, they'll hear back from you on Monday morning; or if they have an urgent request, they'll communicate it with you first instead of just setting an impossible deadline and being upset with you for not meeting it.

Flexibility

I am sure setting your freelance working hours is a helpful tactic, but if you have doubts about its implications on your freedom, rest assured that you have flexibility, too.

As a freelancer, you have the freedom to spoil the schedule from time to time. For instance, if you had a late night out on Wednesday, you can be late for work on Thursday and nobody will ever tell you anything. Or if you want to have a long weekend getaway, skip Friday and work more every day next week to compensate for Friday's absence. Everything is a matter of planning.

Hard Truth #6

You need work principles to succeed.

As I mentioned earlier, you need to have principles to succeed as a freelancer. More importantly, you need to stick with them, no matter what.

If you compromise with yourself once, there will be a second, a third, and a next time. Being a freelancer is about having character. Your clients will respect you and will seek your services *because of* your character and principles; not because you are always available and certainly not because of your low price.

Of course, there will always be clients who'd prefer you said only what they wanted to hear. Those clients will choose the bootlicker contractor and not the freelancer with work principles. The good news is that you don't need such clients anyway.

Think about what matters to *you* and find *your* work principles. As an example, here are a few of mine:

I Need My Freedom

I don't tolerate clients who try to micromanage. They shouldn't try to control when I work, how much I work, where I work, or whether I am on Skype while working. If the client has a good reason to require any of the above information, we can discuss and I can agree, but never just "because I say so." What should matter to the client the most is that I keep my deadlines and do my job well. Freedom is what I couldn't have at my regular office job, but it's what I can afford to *require* as a freelancer. So I do.

I Should Never Ever Have to Lie

Honesty and frankness define me very much as a person. Sometimes, it's a curse but more often, it saves me from trouble in the long run. I don't work with clients and don't take on projects which would compromise my integrity in some way. This is also the reason why I decline projects for marketing products or services which I would not buy and use myself.

I Need to Be Trusted

I believe in the proverb "trust but verify." That's why I don't mind filing regular reports, taking part in weekly meetings and discussions, etc. However, I do have a problem if someone's constantly watching over my shoulder and following every little step along the way. After all, the client is paying for my services, right? The best thing to do is just let me do my job.

I Work Only with Professional Clients

Without a second thought I decline work from people who don't know what they want or even worse, who think they are the smartest people who ever lived and that they know better and can do better than everyone else. These clients often have condescending attitudes and hire freelancers not because they need help, but because you need the job.

These clients are a lost cause. I used to be lured by attractive offers—highly paid projects, a quick job for more than the usual money, interesting product, etc. At the end of the day, I learned my lesson. It is always better, both for my pocket and for my health, to stay away from unprofessional clients.

Effective Communication Is Non-Negotiable

I believe effective communication is a must for a successful collaboration. There's no way a project would be completed successfully, unless the client and the freelancer(s) communicate well. For that reason, I leave my personal relations and ego at the door.

Both the client and the freelancer should ask questions and the other side should answer in a timely manner. The client should give prompt and objective feedback for the job done and not for the person who's done the job.

There should be a healthy team environment. It should be clear that if the freelancer needs help or advice, all he or she should do is ask. And vice versa, if the client has any doubts, concerns, or just needs more details about the project progress, all they need to do is ask.

A Final Thought about Work Principles

I'd like to end this section about having work principles with the following:

I build my reputation on professionalism, skills, happy clients, and trust. I have been disappointed only with colleagues and freelancers who have not developed work principles and have been chasing quick money and temporary results instead.

So my advice to you, fellow freelancers, is to think carefully what you want to achieve as a freelancer.

Figure out what is important to you and build work principles. Then stand your ground when negotiating with clients.

Hard Truth #7

Freelancers make mistakes and you will too. Here are six of the worst ones.

If you have followed the tips in this book so far, chances are you won't be making any of these mistakes. *However, these six mistakes may prevent you from ever succeeding—that's how important they are.* I don't want to take any chances so I will list them here just in case.

Mistake 1: Not Completing Your Profile

When applying for a nine-to-five job, did you send a halfway done resume? I doubt that. So why not complete your Upwork profile before applying to freelance projects?

The freelance profile, along with your proposal, is the first thing which grabs the potential client's attention. Completing it 100% is a serious advantage, no matter how much of a commonsense tip you think this is.

Mistake 2: Pricing Your Services Too Low

The type and quality of your clients pretty much depends on your price.

If you price your services at $5 per hour, you probably will get unappreciative clients who don't care about quality, sometimes don't pay, and think you should do everything they want when they want it, at no additional cost. All they care about is money. They probably even think you don't deserve it anyway.

If you price your services higher and with regards to your skills, experience, creativity, ideas, what your time is worth, and so on, then you will find very good clients who look for skills, experience, creativity, ideas and who are willing to pay the price your time is worth.

Mistake 3: Not Being Honest

Not saying something can be tolerable sometimes, like when you have taken a skill test for Photoshop and you failed for some reason. That's fine—you don't need to start your proposal with it. It's not cool to lie if a client asks about it.

It is a big mistake not to be honest about your skills and knowledge in your profile overview, in your proposal, during your interview, or in any other case. If you land a job because of a lie about skills and expertise, the client will know you lied soon enough simply because you won't be able to do your job properly. This will lead to wasting both your client's time and yours, his money, and eventually to ruining your reputation.

Mistake 4: Ineffective Communication Skills

I know this is a broad topic but off the top of my head, here are the most common mistakes, related to bad communication, which I see every day:

- **Lack of response**—when you apply for a freelance project and the client replies, it is dead wrong to just not reply. If interested, reply in a timely manner. If not interested or available any more, decline politely. It only takes a few seconds. Never leave an e-mail hanging because if you do, that client will likely never seek your services again.

- **Late responses**—when you get a message from a client, try to reply within one business day. If the client asks a question or something else which would require some technological time for you to research and come up with an answer, then reply back (still within a business day) explaining the situation and that you would need X days to give them the answer they seek. Remember to fit in the number of days you will need to come up with the answer.

- **Dodging or ignoring questions**—when a client asks a question (in the job post, about your proposal, during interview, whenever), don't just pretend they never asked. Ignoring the question won't make the client forget that they have asked it in the first place. To the contrary, the client would most probably feel disappointed that they have put their trust in you as a freelancer. If a client asks you a question in the job post, make sure you address that question in your proposal. Do not leave it for the interview—if you do, chances are you won't make it to the interview at all.

Mistake 5: Not Paying Attention to Detail

It's not a coincidence that the client has asked some questions in their job post; or has specific instructions in it for you to follow when applying. If you can't follow simple instructions to apply to a job post, how can the client expect you to follow their instructions when actually working on their project? Being attentive and addressing all questions or details in the job post can only bring you closer to landing the project.

Mistake 6: Not Asking Questions

When I have filtered candidates for job posts maybe only one out of a hundred candidates has asked questions. It's staggering! Why miss out on such a great opportunity?

Many freelancers think that if they ask questions, they will come across as stupid or incompetent. While in reality, asking questions shows me this candidate has put some thought into the project he or she is applying to. Of course, the questions asked should be on topic and deeply related to the specifics of the freelancer's role or duties in the project, if hired.

Ask two or three of your most pressing questions in the proposal, and if you make it to the interview stage be sure to ask all of your questions before you enter a contract with the client.

Hard Truth #8

To succeed as a freelancer, you need to adopt the right state of mind.

Some people get into freelancing with a somewhat negative attitude. Their state of mind follows a line of thinking similar to these:

- The financial crisis made my life really tough and being a freelancer is not ideal, but I am desperate and ready to work for pennies (that's what freelancing is, right?).

- I am a hard-working highly qualified professional, but nobody wants to hire me. I don't know why, I don't know what else they want …

- I am super-smart but employers never give me a chance, they are stupid like that—not understanding that I am good and they miss on the opportunity to hire me.

Some of these may sound ridiculous, but when looking for freelancers, I have heard every single one of them. Don't be like that, please. If you truly want to succeed as a freelancer, you must shift perspective. Choose to be positive for freelance success.

Yes, I can!

This is your motto, starting today. It doesn't matter who tells you what, how desperate your family is, what your friends think about your freelance venture. You will succeed as a freelancer only if *you* believe you will. Repeat after me: "Yes, I can!" because yes, *you* can.

I seek!

A golden goose won't come if you sit quietly in the corner feeling sorry for yourself. Be proactive—research, be brave, create opportunities. Put yourself in situations when you can shine and stand apart from the crowd.

I want!

Nobody will come to offer you a dream project, at least not when you are starting as a freelancer. For that reason the attitude and state of mind "I can, but nobody gives me a chance" won't cut it. To the contrary.

You have to truly want to change yourself and your life for the better *(yes, being a freelancer will change you and your life)* and you need to be ready and embrace that change.

When you truly want something, you will find a way to make it happen. Even when talking about landing your first contract on Upwork.

Be honest and genuine!

As we established earlier, one of the most common mistakes newbie freelancers make is not being honest about their skills and knowledge. Don't be that guy! Be genuine and honest with yourself and with your prospects. Know your skills and capabilities. Also, know what you can teach yourself when needed and be willing to sacrifice the time needed to do so.

Don't misrepresent yourself, for no reason.

Don't enter negotiations for a new contract with the thought how much the client is willing to pay. Think about what your skills are worth and how much *you* want and deserve to be paid.

Be enthusiastic!

Your prospective client has no idea how many rejection letters you have received so far, so don't approach them with a feeling of defeat. It's important that you don't go looking for projects feeling desperate. You never know which client will give you a try, with whom you will work really well, and with whom you'll develop a long-term relationship. For that reason, always apply with enthusiasm—if you want the job, that is.

Hard Truth #9

Some freelancers cannot succeed on their own. If this is the case with you, find a mentor.

Finding a mentor is easier than you might think. You can pay someone to coach you and help you succeed as a freelancer. You can also pay someone to coach you how to be good at your profession. You can pay someone to do both.

But you can also find a few people for free whom you like and trust and whose advice you value. Those people may not even know they are your mentors. What matters is that you take every bit of wisdom, put it into practice, and ask them questions via e-mail, on their blogs or on social media. Always continue to put that knowledge to practice some more.

The internet offers an infinite source of information so use it. Never stop growing, both personally and professionally. Don't be satisfied with the level you reach, no matter how far. Set your goals and set sails to achieve them.

You are good at what you do, I know. But we live in an ever-changing world so you probably can be even better, wouldn't you say?

Attend webinars. If you want to, go meet some colleagues at an offline event. Read a few more books. Whether you improve existing skills or acquire new ones, the bottom line is that you don't let yourself go. You practice, keep your mind sharp, and maintain the work habits you have. Besides, improving skills will enable you to raise prices.

Last Piece of Homework from Me

It's a big homework assignment, but if you do it now, it will save you a lot of trouble down the road—it will help you on multiple occasions to overcome the urge to quit.

- Write down why you want to be a freelancer— be honest, there's no right or wrong here.

- Find out what inspires you and reminds you why you became a freelancer in the first place. Get back to these when you feel desperate. They can be activities, items or people but get back to them—they will bring up your spirit and help you not to give up in hard times.

- Figure out your work principles and write them down. Get back to them if you feel a client is taking advantage. Don't be afraid to stand your ground and say NO.

- Make sure you don't make the top mistakes the majority of starting freelancers make. Check the list regularly.

- List all the qualities you have that you need to succeed as a freelancer.

- Now list all the qualities that you don't have but still need to succeed as a freelancer— next to each of them, write some ideas how you can acquire them.

- Set your working hours and tell your clients and colleagues.

- Choose what to use for planning your time — e.g. a paper time planner, Google calendar, even a blank notepad could work. Try out a few tools and choose one. Use it on a daily basis.

- Learn how to manage your time and continue improving your time management skills on a daily basis.

- Be positive and proactive. Adopt the right state of mind for freelance success—starting now!

- Find a mentor.

SOME FINAL WORDS...

After reading this book and completing all the homework exercises, you will have *everything* you'd need to start a successful career on Upwork.

Don't be fooled though—this is just the beginning. There's plenty more to be done—from landing your first project, through getting your first five-star review, all the way to winning your first repeat client. Then the time for marketing and networking comes.

You'll learn that the best form of marketing is referrals and word of mouth, but that comes after a while and after a few successfully completed projects. And that is probably a topic for a whole other book.

Being a freelancer is hard. But did you think it would be easy? I don't think there's anything good in life that's easy.

On the bright side—as a freelancer, I know what I am doing and why I am doing it. As a freelancer I can choose my clients and projects. I work only on projects I like and I have fun with; I also work only with people I respect, who I feel good communicating with, and people it is fun to work with. If *I* can do it, *you* can do it!

Becoming a freelancer is hard and takes time—but I gotta tell you, it's worth it 100%.

Be free and prosper!

~Diana

APPENDIX 1: PAYMENT METHODS ON UPWORK

Disclaimer: This appendix is for informational purposes only. It is in no way a representative, exhaustive, or legally-binding document. Fees and regulations widely vary depending on your nationality, country of residence, and location of payment method registration. It is your responsibility to check with local authorities, bank, or third-party service providers to see what regulations or fees may apply in your specific case.

Upwork offers the following payment methods for freelancers to withdraw their hard-earned money— PayPal, Skrill, Payoneer, wire transfer, and direct deposit/ACH.

Depending on your country of residence, some of these payment methods may not be available. Please, <u>check with your Upwork account for options</u>. (see Appendix 2: URL References and note that for the link to work, you need to be logged in to your Upwork account. Otherwise, you will just be redirected to the website log in page and then to your member homepage.)

PayPal

This is one of the most preferred payment methods for freelancers who work online, including myself. It is easy to set up and often most cost effective for non-US freelancers when withdrawing money from Upwork.

For every withdrawal, Upwork charges a $1 fee. PayPal doesn't charge anything if your PayPal default currency is USD. Otherwise, it will charge a 2.5% currency conversion fee.

You can register with PayPal at paypal.com.

If located in the US, you can also apply for a PayPal Prepaid MasterCard. You can use it to shop online, make payments in stores, or do ATM withdrawals.

If you are located outside the US and want to spend your money off PayPal, you need to add and verify a bank account, VISA, or VISA Electron card. Only then you will be able to withdraw money from your PayPal account to your bank. Search PayPal's HELP section for instructions how to add a bank account or a card to your account and verify it. If you need further assistance, contact their support.

For every withdrawal from PayPal to a bank account or a card, PayPal has always charged me $2.50. However, fees vary depending on location and type of account, so please, check with your PayPal account and bank for specific fees.

Skrill

This has been my backup payment method on Upwork since the beginning of my freelance practice. It's easy to setup and suitable for international payments. It is a bit more expensive than PayPal because Skrill recently increased their fees.

For every withdrawal, Upwork charges a $1 fee. Skrill doesn't charge anything if your Skrill default currency is USD. Otherwise, it may charge a currency conversion fee.

You can register with Skrill at skrill.com.

Similarly to PayPal, you need to verify a bank account, VISA, or VISA Electron card with Skrill so that you are able to withdraw money from your Skrill account to your bank, and so you will also be able to spend it off Skrill.

For every withdrawal from Skrill to my bank, Skrill used to charge $2.50. However, I have not used it this way in a while and don't know if the fee is accurate. Besides, fees vary depending on different factors so please, check with your Skrill account and your bank for specific fees.

If you are a resident of a country in the European Union, you can also apply for a Skrill Prepaid MasterCard and use it to spend the money in your Skrill account without first transferring it to your bank.

Payoneer

This is an especially handy payment method for freelancers outside the US. When you register with Payoneer, you can get a Payoneer Prepaid MasterCard but also a bank account with Bank of America through Payoneer's Global Payment Service.

Like with PayPal and Skrill, fees and terms of use vary depending on your country of residence so be sure to check what options apply in your specific situation.

Upwork charges a $2 per withdrawal to your Payoneer Prepaid MasterCard. It is free to receive money on your Payoneer Prepaid MasterCard within two business days. If you want an instant withdrawal, Payoneer charges a $2.50 fee.

You can register with Payoneer at Payoneer.com.

You can use your Payoneer Prepaid MasterCard like any other debit or credit bank card to shop online, pay in stores via POS terminals, or make ATM withdrawals. Please, check with your account or customer support what fees apply in your country.

Wire Transfers

This payment method requires the addition of your bank account information to your Upwork account. Upwork offers two types of wire transfers—local funds/currency transfer and USD currency wire transfer.

• Local Currency/Funds Transfer

Upwork charges a flat fee for Local Funds Transfers (LFT) which varies from $0.99 to $4.99 depending on the country and bank account information.

Additional fees may apply on your bank's side. Please, check with your bank for details.

• USD Wire Transfer

Upwork charges a flat fee of $30 per USD Wire Transfer.

Note that your bank may charge additional fees for receiving such a transfer. Fees vary by country, bank and currency so please, check with your bank how much it would cost to receive a USD wire transfer from Upwork.

Direct Deposit/ACH

Upwork requires a US bank account in order to use this payment method. They do not charge a fee. Please, check with your bank if additional fees apply to receive money from Upwork through direct deposit/ACH.

These are all available payment methods for freelancers on Upwork. For more details about any of the options, additional requirements (if any), associated costs and links to corresponding third-party websites, please visit Upwork Payment Methods Options page (see Appendix 2: URL References).

APPENDIX 2: URL REFERENCE

Here's a list of all URL addresses used in this book with their respective numbers, in the order of their appearance:

Page 4—My Upwork profile—
https://www.upwork.com/fl/dianamarinova

Page 4—My LinkedIn profile—
https://www.linkedin.com/in/dianamarinovafreelance

Page 4—My website and freelance marketing blog—
http://www.dianamarinova.com/

Page 5—Upwork about page—
https://www.upwork.com/about/

Page 22—Upwork's best practices tips for choosing your profile photo—
https://www.upwork.com/blog/2014/10/how-to-guide-perfect-profile-picture/

Page 33—Upwork's requirements for videos on profiles—https://support.upwork.com/hc/en-us/articles/211063218-What-type-of-video-should-I-include-on-my-profile-

Page 48—Sales & Marketing category of Upwork (profiles)—
https://www.upwork.com/o/profiles/browse/c/sales-marketing/

Page 48--Sales & Marketing category (jobs)—
https://www.upwork.com/o/jobs/browse/c/sales-marketing/

Page 49—Search engine on Upwork—
https://www.upwork.com/i/freelancer-categories/

Page 90—Upwork Plus account—
https://support.upwork.com/hc/en-
us/articles/211062888-Membership-Plans-Basic-Plus

Page 93—Here's a checklist I give away to my
community—http://www.dianamarinova.com/wp-
content/uploads/2015/05/Dianas-Ideal-Prospective-
Client-Checklist.pdf

Page 151—My Google Calendar—
http://www.dianamarinova.com/how-to-use-google-
calendar-for-better-time-management/

Page 177—Payment methods available in your Upwork
account—https://www.upwork.com/disbursement-
methods

Page 181—Upwork Payment Methods Options page—
https://support.upwork.com/hc/en-
us/articles/211063728-Payment-Methods-Options

ACKNOWLEDGMENTS

I have so many people to thank for their support. To everyone who stood by me during the past few years as I was making a name for myself as a freelancer. Thank you for the continuous encouragement while I was writing my first book.

I am eternally grateful to my partner in life and business, Yordan Dimov, without whom I might have not taken the road of a freelancer. He taught me how to free myself from traditional thinking. He helped me see there is so much more to life than the rat race and the ordinary life the majority of people lead. He reminded me how much I love traveling. He pushed me toward making my dreams come true. He believed in me when I didn't.

To my friends and family who always supported me. They brought to me inspiration, and reminded me in tough times that if I truly wanted to make my dreams come true, I should simply keep at it.

To my clients—for believing in me in the first place and helping me grow professionally and personally.

To my blog readers, a global community of freelancers from all over the world, whose invaluable feedback not only prompted me to write this book, but whose readership also keeps me going and planning future books, training courses, and blog posts to help starting and experienced freelancers alike make their dreams come true.

Thanks to my editor, Jeri Walker from JeriWB Word Bank Writing & Editing at jeriwb.com, who made sure this book brings as much value to starting freelancers as possible.

Thank you all for helping me succeed. Through this book, you will be helping many others succeed in their lives as well.

ABOUT DIANA MARINOVA

Born and raised in a small country in Eastern Europe, today Diana Marinova fully enjoys the freelance lifestyle.

She wears many hats—freelance marketing consultant, blogger, freelance mentor, start-up enthusiast, but above all—traveler by heart.

What Diana loves most about freelancing is the opportunity to be the master of her own time and life. Working online enables her to make a living without being bound to any given place or time. She cherishes the opportunity to make a good living while still having time for hobbies and trotting the globe one step at a time.

She strongly believes everybody deserves the chance to live their dream life. That's why she writes books, runs a blog, and dedicates a significant portion of her time to helping fellow freelancers succeed.

This is Diana's first published book:

Diana's Freelance Tips: How to Succeed on Upwork
A Winning 7-Step Formula & Some Hard Truths from a
Freelance Pro

Her book is the direct result of extensive experience as a freelance marketing consultant and the many questions her blog readers ask on a daily basis.

More than forty of Diana's freelance projects have received the maximum five-star rating for a total of 6,500+ paid hours on Upwork. She has the expertise to walk you through the process of laying a solid foundation for a successful freelance practice. She shows you how to start from zero and reach as far as you want as a freelancer.

You can learn more about her and tap into her experience through the 150+ posts available on her blog. You can join her growing community of freelancers to get free resources and updates.

Join at www.dianamarinova.com/join-email-list.

Made in the USA
Lexington, KY
04 July 2017